New Concepts in
Paper Quilling

New Concepts in
Paper Quilling
Techniques for Cards and Gifts

MARIE BROWNING

STERLING

New York / London
www.sterlingpublishing.com

Prolific Impressions Production Staff:

Editor in Chief: Mickey Baskett
Copy Editor: Phyllis Mueller
Graphics: Dianne Miller, Karen Turpin
Styling: Lenos Key
Photography: Jerry Mucklow of Rocket Photography, Visions West Photography
Administration: Jim Baskett

Library of Congress Cataloging-in-Publication Data

Browning, Marie.
  New concepts in paper quilling : techniques for cards & gifts / Marie Browning.
      p. cm.
  Includes index.
  ISBN-13: 978-1-4027-3510-3
  ISBN-10: 1-4027-3510-3
  1. Paper quillwork. I. Title.

TT870.B757 2008
745.54--dc22

                                        2007026872

4 6 8 10 9 7 5 3

Published by Sterling Publishing Co., Inc.
387 Park Avenue South, New York, NY 10016
© 2008 by Prolific Impressions, Inc.
Distributed in Canada by Sterling Publishing
c/o Canadian Manda Group, 165 Dufferin Street,
Toronto, Ontario, Canada M6K 3H6
Distributed in the United Kingdom by GMC Distribution Services,
Castle Place, 166 High Street, Lewes, East Sussex, England BN7 1XU
Distributed in Australia by Capricorn Link (Australia) Pty. Ltd.
P.O. Box 704, Windsor, NSW 2756, Australia

Printed in China
All rights reserved

ISBN-13: 978-104027-3510-3
ISBN-10: 1-4027-3510-3

For information about custom editions, special sales, premium and corporate purchases, please contact Sterling Special Sales Department at 800-805-5489 or specialsales@sterlingpub.com.

Acknowledgments

I thank these manufacturers for their generous contributions of quality products and support.

For glues for all surfaces:
Beacon Adhesives, Mt. Vernon, NY, USA, www.beaconcreates.com

For swirl flower rubber stamps and paper sculpture tools:
Coronado Island Designs, Coronado, CA, USA, www.cistamping.com

For cutting tools, Cloud 9 Design decorative papers, and scrapbook embellishments and stickers:
Fiskars Brands, Inc., Wausau, WI, USA, www.fiskars.com

For decorative buttons, charms, and beads:
Jesse James & Co., Allentown, PA, USA, www.dressitup.com

For decorative papers, scrapbook embellishments, and stickers:
K & Company, Parkville, MO, USA, www.kandcompany.com

For charms, rubber stamps, and peel-off stickers:
Magenta, Sainte-Julie, QC, Canada, www.magentastyle.com

For window cards, acrylic paints, acrylic varnishes, and dimensional varnish:
Plaid Enterprises Inc., Norcross, GA, USA, www.plaidonline.com

For paper crafts and quilling supplies, including husking boards and patterns:
Alli and Dave Bartkowski, Quilled Creations, Penfield, NY, USA, www.quilledcreations.com

For inkpads:
Tsukineko Co., Redmond, WA, USA, www.tsukineko.com

About the Author

MARIE BROWNING

Marie Browning is a consummate craft designer who has made a career of designing products, writing books and articles, and teaching and demonstrating. You may have been charmed by her creative acumen but not been aware of the woman behind it; she has designed stencils, stamps, transfers, and a variety of other award-winning product lines for art and craft supply companies. As well as writing numerous books on creative living (with over one million copies currently in print), Marie's articles and designs have appeared in numerous home decor and crafts magazines.

Marie Browning earned a Fine Arts Diploma from Camosun College, where she serves on a program advisory board in the Visual Arts department, and attended the University of Victoria. She is a design member of the Crafts and Hobby Association (CHA) and chair of the CHA Designer Trend Committee, which researches and writes about upcoming trends in the arts and crafts industry. In 2004 Marie was selected by *Craftrends* trade publication as a "Top Influential Industry Designer."

She lives, gardens, and crafts on Vancouver Island in Canada. She and her husband Scott have three children: Katelyn, Lena, and Jonathan. Marie can be contacted at www.mariebrowning.com.

Books by Marie Browning Published by Sterling

Creative Collage: Making Memories in Mixed Media (2007)
Paper Crafts Workshop: A Beginner's Guide to Techniques & Projects (2007)
Paper Crafts Workshop: Traditional Card Techniques (2007)
Metal Crafting Workshop (2006)
Casting for Crafters (2006)
Paper Mosaics in an Afternoon (2006)
Snazzy Jars (2006)
Jazzy Gift Baskets (2006)
Purse Pizzazz (2005)
Really Jazzy Jars (2005)
Totally Cool Polymer Clay for Kids (2005)
Totally Cool Soapmaking for Kids (2004 – re-printed in softcover)
Wonderful Wraps (2003 – re-printed in softcover)

Jazzy Jars (2003 – re-printed in softcover)
Designer Soapmaking (2003 – re-printed in German)
300 Recipes for Soap (2002 – re-printed in softcover and in French and Chinese)
Crafting with Vellum and Parchment (2001 – re-printed in softcover as *New Paper Crafts*)
Melt and Pour Soaps (2000 – re-printed in softcover)
Hand Decorating Paper (2000 – re-printed in softcover)
Memory Gifts (2000 – re-printed in soft-cover as *Family Photocrafts*)
Making Glorious Gifts from your Garden (1999 – re-printed in softcover)
Handcrafted Journals, Albums, Scrapbooks & More (1999 – re-printed in softcover)
Beautiful Handmade Natural Soaps (1998 – re-printed in softcover as *Natural Soapmaking*)

Table of Contents

JEWELRY PROJECTS 118

HOME DECOR & GIFT PROJECTS 92

METRIC CONVERSION CHART 127
INDEX 127

The Art & Craft of Quilling

Quilling is the art of rolling very thin strips of paper into scroll shapes and creating artistic designs with the various shapes, which are glued onto a base. Quilling is also known as **paper filigree** or **paper scroll work**.

The delicate paper craft of quilling is based on coiling and arranging strips of paper. It's the arranging – what you do with the coils and how you put them together – that turns them into art. A quilled design can be simple, containing a few coils, or it can be a complex masterpiece containing hundreds of individual coils and scrolls. Getting started in quilling is easy and inexpensive. It requires a few specialized tools and easy-to-learn skills. Quilling is suitable for any age group and can be as simple or complex as you wish.

The quilled creations in this book incorporate other paper crafts techniques such as fringing, crimping, and shaped paper flowers. While not technically quilling, swirl flowers and punched, shaped flowers and leaves add dimension and interest to quilled arrangements. Another technique is husking, which uses the paper quilling strips in a novel way to create paper shapes.

Simple quilled cards can be made rather quickly, but many designs take longer. More involved pieces can take hours of patient work, which seems to be the attraction to this additive paper craft. If you appreciate creating unique, carefully handmade cards and gifts, you will quickly be drawn into the charms of quilling and will soon be creating keepsakes that are sure to be valued heirlooms.

Quilling is a time-honored, elegant paper craft that is popular again. Everyone wants to learn how to quill! In response, companies are introducing exciting new papers and the Internet has made it easy to find what you need. I have filled this book with a variety of new designs for cards, home decor and gift items, and jewelry that take very little time so you can introduce yourself to this fun and inexpensive craft.

Marie Browning

A little bit of history

Quilling, in different forms and wrought with various materials, is an old craft that has appeared in many different cultures throughout history. In the 4th and 5th centuries, extremely intricate, lacelike filigree work of fine gold and silver wire was found on ancient pillars, vases, and tombs in various parts of Europe. By the 13th century, artists mimicked this look with strips of paper, rolled loosely, placed on edge, and gilded to resemble precious metal. (Supposedly even experts were fooled at first glance.) During this period, paper filigree was almost exclusively the work of nuns and monks who used it to decorate religious articles. The art of paper quilling, inspired by the earlier ornate metal filigree, was an affordable alternative to delicate gold and silver wirework.

It is widely believed the name quilling is derived from the feather quills said to have been used to roll the paper strips. Others claim that once the strips of paper are curled and released, they resemble a row of barbs on a feather, or quill.

Samples of Chinese filigree jewelry. These labor-intensive, handcrafted pieces are made of sterling silver and gold wire along with semi-precious stones. The techniques used to make them are similar to the filigree wire pieces that inspired paper quilling. These samples, some of which date from the 1920s, and are from Elle of California, a seller of unique and collectible jewelry.

Quilling came to North America in the 18th century about the time of the American Revolution. It was a craft practiced by rich ladies when paper itself was a scarce luxury. In the 18th century, paper filigree work became popular in England and was taught along with needlework as a proper pastime for fashionable young ladies. *New Lady Magazine* described filigree as "the art which affords an amusement to the female mind capable of the most pleasing and extensive variety." Many times quillwork was combined with shells, wax flowers, twisted wire, and chipped mica, which added a sparkling effect to designs viewed in candlelight.

Due to the fragile nature of the materials, few very old pieces remain, although the collections of many museums in the New England area of the United States include at least a few examples from the 1700s and 1800s. After the early 19th century, no notable works of quilling appeared, and the craft seemed a nearly lost art. Quilling again became a popular paper craft in 1950. Today, as paper crafts grow in popularity, quilling, too, is enjoying a revival. Modern quilled designs often are combined with other paper sculpture techniques to create astonishingly beautiful cards and framed art.

Basic Supplies & Tools

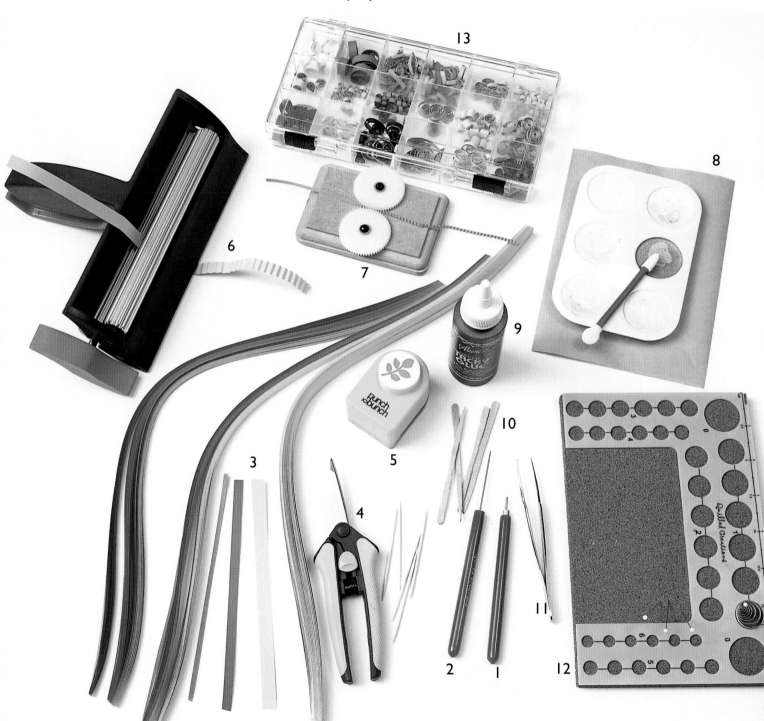

Pictured above: 1) quilling tool; 2) needle tool; 3) paper strips – ⅛", ¼", ⅜"; 4) scissors; 5) decorative paper punch; 6) large paper crimper; 7) paper crimper designed for quilling strips; 8) watercolors; 9) white glue; 10) toothpicks, flat and round; 11) tweezers; 12) quilling board with pins; 13) storage container for quilled shapes.

Quilling Tool

A quilling tool has a metal end with a tiny slot in the middle that's mounted on a plastic or wooden handle. It makes it easy for beginners to roll the paper strips and create quilling shapes. The slotted quilling tool is preferred for making long coils, such as those required for the bell shape, because it's easier to keep the coil even over a longer length of paper.

To use a quilling tool:

1. Tear off a strip of quilling paper to the specific length. Slip the end of the paper into the slot and start rolling. Place the paper just inside the slot – any overhang will create a tiny tag in the middle of the quilled shape. TIP: It's easier to insert the paper if you hold it at a 45-degree angle to the tool.
2. Begin to roll the paper, using your fingers to maintain even tension and keep the strip even. You can roll the paper towards you or away from you; you will immediately discover what direction is natural for you.
3. When you reach the end of the paper strip, give the tool a one-quarter turn in the opposite direction to loosen it, and gently remove the coil. Simply let it expand to the size you want and glue the tail to secure.

Needle Tool

Many artists prefer a pointed end tool, like a paper piercer, to quill paper. It is a little harder to master, but it makes a finer center hole in the shapes and tighter rolls. The needle tool is also used to make spirals.

You can use a **round wooden toothpick** or a **large corsage pin** to make coils in the same way you would use a needle tool, making it easy to share the craft with others.

To use a needle tool:

1. Tear off a strip of quilling paper to the specified length. Slightly moisten one end of the strip and place the strip against your index finger. Place the pointed end of the tool on top of the end of the moistened strip. Place your thumb on top of the tool.
2. With the paper and tool between your index finger and thumb, roll the paper around the tool, using your thumb. Keep the edges of the strip as even as possible as you roll the paper strip around the point of the tool.
3. Remove the tool from the coil by simply pulling it out.

Quilling Papers

Pre-cut paper strips ⅛" wide and 24" long are the most popular size for quilling. However, many other sizes are available. Look for ¹⁄₁₆", ⅜", ¼", ½", ⅝", ¾" and 1" widths. The ¹⁄₁₆" strips are used to make quilled designs in watches; ⅜" strips are perfect for fringed flowers. Quilling strips used for the projects in this book include ⅛", ¼", and ⅜" sizes.

Quilling paper strips are readily available at craft stores and come in a huge range of colors and types. They can be solid-color strips, graduated strips, center-graduated strips, two-toned strips, and metallic colored strips.

You can also make **your own specialized and custom strips**. You need to be very accurate – the strip's width should be the same along its entire length. Use a paper trimmer and thin paper when cutting your own strips.

Scissors

Sharp, pointy scissors are what you need for trimming coils or for fringing. I especially like **spring-loaded ergonomic scissors** for easy, fast fringing.

Decorative Punches

Leaf, branch, and flower motif punches can be used to quickly add foliage or paper sculptured flowers to quilled arrangements. Shape leaves and petals on a **soft foam pad** with an **embossing tool** to create dimension before adding them to arrangements.

Paper Crimper

A **paper crimper** adds another dimension to the paper strips before quilling for a fanciful effect. Use a regular crimper for both quilling strips and paper panels. You can find small crimpers especially designed for ⅛" quilling strips at crafts and paper arts stores.

Continued on next page

Continued from page 11.

Watercolors (Interference or Shimmering Metallic)

A light brushing of glistening paint adds a beautiful glimmer to quilled designs. Apply **watercolor paint** to the shapes after they have been glued to the base. Use the foam applicator that comes with the paints or the kind of foam applicator used for applying makeup. Use very little moisture so you do not warp the paper shapes.

White Craft Glue

The best adhesive for quilling is **quick-drying white liquid glue** that dries clear. I like to pour the glue into a small disposable container and apply it with a toothpick. Stir the glue often or put a damp sponge over the top of the container to keep the glue from forming a film or drying out. (The sponge is also handy for keeping your fingers clean and free of glue.) TIP: Use a very small amount of glue when ending or joining your shaped coils – too much glue may show and spoil the look of your project.

Glue Gun

A **hot glue gun** is used when creating swirl flowers and for gluing punched and shaped paper pieces.

Wooden Toothpicks

Use **flat toothpicks** for applying glue and **round toothpicks** for rolling paper strips.

Tweezers

A good pair of **tweezers** is important for placing paper coils. Use tweezers with sharp points for best results. Here's how: Hold the coil with tweezers, apply a small amount of glue to the bottom edges, and position.

Tweezers are also used when creating eccentric coils to pull the centers of coils to the edge and for holding paper strips together tightly while glue dries.

Quilling Board

Although not essential, a **quilling board** is very handy for creating coils of the same size and for holding coils while glue dries. Here's how: Place the rolled paper strip in the recessed hole of the board – the coil will release to the proper size. Use a pin to hold the loop to one side as you glue the end of the strip.

You can also use a **corkboard** to pin and hold the coils while they dry.

Pins

Use **regular straight pins** to hold your pieces together while the glue dries. Purchase rustproof pins with small glass heads for best results. Pins are also helpful for securing an arrangement when you want to set it aside to finish later.

Embellishments

Some of my favorite embellishments for quilled designs include rhinestones (buy them in sticker form or apply with white glue), metallic peel-off stickers, and mini pom-poms for flower centers.

Work Space

A clean, well-lighted area is important when quilling. A **lamp** that mimics natural light is a good investment for this intricate work. Take frequent breaks and stretch your hands to avoid cramping.

tips: STORING SUPPLIES & QUILLED SHAPES

Long, loose paper strips can quickly become damaged if they are not stored properly. I sort my strips by width and color and store them in their original plastic bag, held closed with a paper clamp. If you have space, hang up the bags for easy access.

I keep finished coils in segmented plastic containers sorted by size, type, and color. When I create coils and shapes for projects, I usually make a few extra of each one just in case. If I don't use them, these extra pieces are ready to use on other projects.

The Quilling Technique

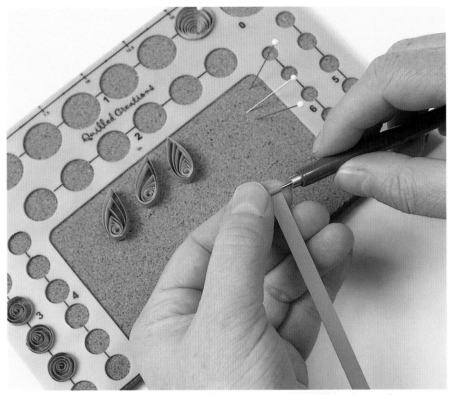

Starting to curl a paper strip. A quilling board can be seen in the background.

Create all your coils and shape them according to the instructions. As you go, pin the shapes to a quilling board to keep them organized. If there are patterns available, place a copy of the pattern on a corkboard, cover with a piece of wax paper, and pin the pieces in place.

4. **Arrange:** Arrange the quilled shapes on your project base, using tweezers to pick up and place the quilled shapes. (Using tweezers prevents you from mishandling and distorting the quilled shape.)
5. **Glue the shapes:** When you are happy with the arrangement, use very little white glue to glue the coils together at the sides to create the designs.
6. **Attach:** To attach the quilled designs to the base, use a toothpick to apply a thin layer of glue to the bottom of the finished shape. Position on the base and allow to dry. ❏

1. **Prepare:** Choose your design, read the instructions carefully to make sure you have everything you need, and gather your supplies and tools.
2. **Tear:** Measure the paper strips with a ruler and tear the strips to the lengths specified in the project instructions. A torn edge can be glued better than a cut edge and will not create an obvious seam.
3. **Roll:** Start the first coil by threading the end of a paper strip through the slot in the metal tip of the quilling tool. (TIP: Hold the tool at an angle to the paper strip for easy threading.) Slide the tool to the very end of the strip and start to roll. Use your index and middle fingers to help guide the paper. Keep rolling until you reach the end of the strip. Move the tool a quarter twist back toward you. Gently wiggle the tool and pull it out of the coil.

    For a loose coil, set down the coil and release it. Pick up the coil, adjust the size, and put a tiny dot of glue inside the end. Press the end and hold for a few seconds to allow the glue to dry. *For a tight coil,* leave the paper strip on the tool and glue the tail.

tips: QUILLING

- The tighter you roll the paper, the smaller the shape will be.
- To make large shapes, glue two quilling strips together, end to end. They can be the same color or two different colors.
- Be sure your coils are rolled evenly. I usually put my finger over the top as I roll to keep the edges even.
- Use very little glue – that's all you need to hold the pieces together.
- A needle tool creates a very fine hole in the center of tight coils; the slotted tool produces a tiny bent piece in the center. Always roll your quilling paper as close to the end as possible to minimize this crease.

Basic Quilled Shapes

There are many quilled shapes that are possible. However, you only need to know how to make a few shapes to be able to make a wide variety of quilled designs and cards. The names of the shapes often vary within the quilling community. I have labeled the examples of the shapes with the names I used for the projects in this book and have included alternate names in parentheses with the descriptions of the shapes. With these basic shapes, you will be able to create a variety of designs. The circle – the shape that comes off the tool – is the basis of all the other shapes. The circle size depends on the length of the paper strip and how tightly it is rolled.

See examples of shapes on pages 15, & 17

Tight Coil (Peg)

Roll the strip. Glue closed while the strip is still on quilling tool and the coil is tight. Remove carefully. Tight coils can be used as a design element or glued under another shape to raise it and create dimension.

Loose Coil

Roll the strip, remove it from the quilling tool, and let it open. Place it in circle template on a quilling board for a uniform size. Place a small amount of glue at the end to close. The loose coil is the most common quilling shape; it's pinched and manipulated to create all the others.

Loose Scroll

Roll the strip, remove it from quilling tool, and it let open. (The tail is not glued.)

Eccentric Coil (Off-Center Coil)

Make a loose coil. Place it in a circle template on a quilling board. Allow it to expand. Glue the end. Using tweezers or a straight pin, pull the center of the coil off to the side and pin it to the board. Place a small amount of glue on top of the coiled edges to hold. Let dry, remove from the board, and make the shape. Place the glue side down when arranging.

Eccentric Teardrop

Make an eccentric coil. Pinch the bottom of the coil to form the teardrop shape.

Oval

Make a loose coil. Squeeze gently into an oval shape without creasing the ends.

Square

Make a loose coil. Pinch the four corners of the outer circle to create a square.

Teardrop

Make a loose coil. Pinch one end of the circle to form the teardrop shape.

Petal

Make a loose coil. Pinch one end of the circle to form the teardrop shape. As you pinch, twist slightly to make the curved petal.

Eye (Marquis Coil)

Make a loose coil. Pinch both ends of the circle to make the eye shape.

Leaf

Make a loose coil. Pinch both ends of the circle, making an eye shape. As you pinch, twist the ends slightly to make the curved leaf shape.

Continued on page 16

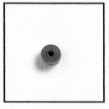 Tight Coil

 Teardrop

 Loose Coil

 Petal

 Loose Scroll

 Eye

 Eccentric Coil

 Leaf

 Eccentric Teardrop

 Diamond

 Oval

 Half Moon

 Square

 Heart

Continued from page 14.

Diamond

Make a loose coil. Pinch two opposite sides while pinching the middle points to form the diamond.

Half Moon

Make a loose coil. Pinch on two sides while placing your finger in the middle of one side. (This will cause an indentation to create the half moon shape.)

Heart

Pinch one end as you would to make a teardrop. Hold the pinched end in one hand while you push the other end towards the center to form the heart.

Multicolor Coil (Two-Strip Coil)

Make this coil by rolling two strips of different colors at the same time. TIP: If you're using a quilling tool, offset the paper strips ¼" at the beginning; two thicknesses of paper won't fit in the slot.

Multicolor Coil (Glued-Strip Coil)

Glue a strip of one color to the end of a strip of another color. Use as many colors as you want and roll as usual.

Crimp (Waves)

For small waves, run the strip through a paper crimper. Roll the crimped strip into a loose coil and shape as you would uncrimped paper strips.

Single Scroll

Roll the strip. Remove from the quilling tool and let open into a loose scroll. Don't glue the tail. Using the point of the tool, uncurl the end to the desired length.

V-Scroll

Fold the strip in half to crease. Roll the ends on the outside of the paper away from the center crease.

Feeler Scroll

For a single feeler, roll only a small part of the paper strip on one end, leaving the rest of the strip straight. Double feelers can be made with the strip folded in half (like the example pictured).

T-Scroll

Make a feeler scroll. Glue the inside "legs" together.

Quotes

Fold a strip in half. Roll the ends in the same direction – one toward the center crease, the other away from it.

S-Scroll

Roll both ends of the paper strip to the middle on opposite sides. Try not to crease the middle of the paper.

Scrolled Heart (Open Heart)

Fold the strip of paper in half. Roll the ends toward the center of the crease to form the heart.

Scissors Curl

To make a slight curl in a paper strip, hold the scissors blade and paper strip flat against your thumb, then gently pull the strip to curl it. Repeat to make a curlier strip. TIP: Hold the scissors blade gently to avoid ripping the paper.

Spiral (Twist or Tendril)

Roll the paper strip in a spiral around a needle tool or toothpick.

Harp

Glue several strips of paper together at the ends. Twist and fan the strips to form shapes. Glue at the ends and where strips touch to secure the shapes.

Bell

Make a tight coil, rolling slightly off-center to form the bell. Glue closed while still on quilling tool. Remove from the tool. Use a sharp pencil or round toothpick to adjust the shape. TIP: Paint the inside of the bell with glue to make sure the form is secure.

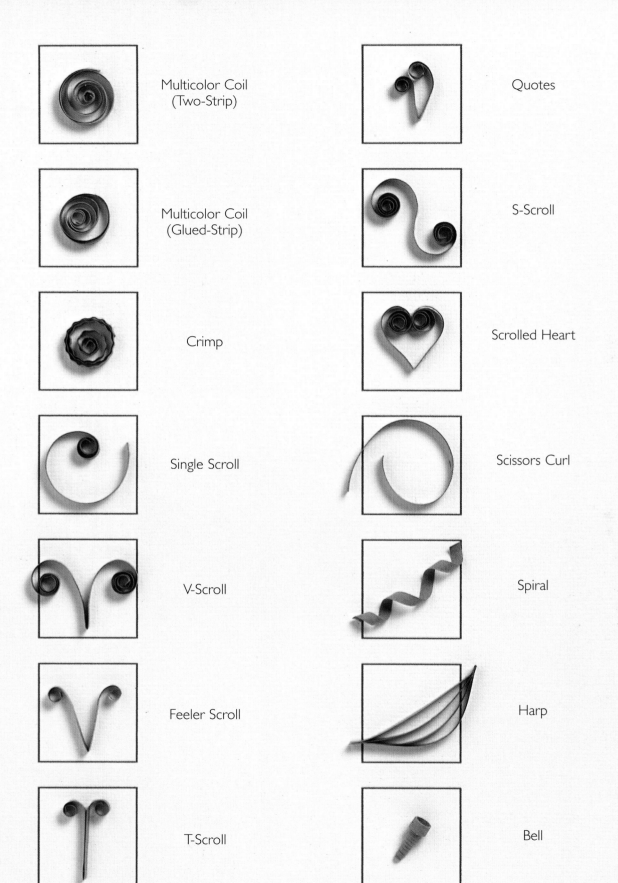

Multicolor Coil
(Two-Strip)

Quotes

Multicolor Coil
(Glued-Strip)

S-Scroll

Crimp

Scrolled Heart

Single Scroll

Scissors Curl

V-Scroll

Spiral

Feeler Scroll

Harp

T-Scroll

Bell

Making Fringed Flowers

Fringed flowers are made from paper strips that were cut to look like fringe, rolled, and glued. A basic fringed flower is made with a paper strip 6" long. You can cut the strip shorter or longer to vary the flower size.

Basic Supplies & Tools

- Quilling paper strips, ⅜" (¼" and ¾" paper strips can also be used; variegated quilling papers are especially nice)
- Sharp scissors with short blades, for cutting
- Quilling tool, to coil and wrap the centers and petals
- Pencil and ruler, for marking and measuring
- White glue
- *Optional:*

Fringing machine – Although they are expensive, these small machines cut ⅜" strips into fringes evenly and quickly. If you are planning to make lots of fringed flower designs, this tool is recommended.

Decorative edge scissors, for cutting designs in the edges of strips prior to fringing

Supplies for Fringing – 1) Scissors, 2) fringing machine, 3) quilling strips, 4) fringed strips, 5) fringed flowers, 6) quilling tool, 7) decorative edge scissors

Creating Flowers

Here's how to make a fringed flower without a fringing machine.

1. Cut a ⅜" paper strip 6" long (or your desired length).
2. For easier fringing, draw a light pencil line ⅛" from one long edge of the paper strip. Use this line as a cutting guide. (As you become more comfortable with the technique, you will not need a pencil line.)
3. Make small cuts at a 90-degree angle along one edge of the paper strip up to the cutting guideline. Make the cuts very close together and evenly spaced.
4. After the strip is fringed, roll it up into a tight coil and glue the end.
5. Holding the flower between both thumbs and index fingers, peel the fringed petals outward with your thumbs. Voila! A fringed flower!

Creating Flower Centers

Same-color Centers:
Don't fringe 1" to 2" at the beginning of the strip. Trim the un-fringed length of the strip to ⅛" wide. Start the roll from the narrow end – this will form a tight center for the flower.

Different-color Centers:
Glue a ⅛" quilling strip 1" to 2" long to the bottom (uncut) edge of the fringed strip. Start rolling from this end to form a tight colored center in the flower. (See photo.)

Examples

1 – Fringed flower

2 – Fringed flower with different color center

3 – Fringed bud

Making a different-colored center for a fringed flower.

Creating a Fringed Bud

1. Roll a 3" length of ⅜" fringed quilling paper to form a smaller, narrower fringed flower.
2. Make a bell shape with a 3" piece of green ⅛" quilling paper.
3. Glue the bell shape to the underside of the fringed bud. Glue to the project.

Pictured above: "Flowers in the Windows Card," See page 65 for instructions.

Making Swirl Flowers

These three-dimensional paper flowers are a wonderful addition to quilled arrangements, and using the specially designed rubber stamps makes it easy to create these miniature beauties. For an endless variety of blooms, try changing the paper size, ink colors, decorative scissors, and spiral stamp size.

Basic Supplies & Tools

- Card stock (in flower colors)
- Spiral flower rubber stamps (available in five sizes for making flowers ½" to 1" in diameter)
- Inkpads (in flower colors)
- Scissors
- Decorative edge scissors
- Hemostat (metal clamp)
- Glue gun with clear glue sticks

How to

1. Using a spiral flower stamp and inkpad, stamp a sheet of flowers on card stock.
2. With decorative scissors, cut from the outside to the center, following the spiral design. (Photo 1) Hold the scissors in one place and move the paper, feeding it into the blades. When you reposition the scissors blades to make another cut, line up the cut motifs with the blades so they fit like puzzle pieces.
3. Clamp the hemostat (metal clamp) on the outside tip of the cut paper spiral. Remove your fingers from the clamp handles and, holding the stem of the tool, roll the paper around the clamp towards the center of the swirl, keeping the edges even. (Photo 2)
4. Open the jaws of the metal clamp and gently remove the rolled paper strip. Let it open into a flower shape.
5. Adjust the bloom as desired. (Photo 3)
6. Turn over the flower. Hold the flower so you can see the hole in the middle. Apply a generous drop of hot glue and press the base at the center to cover the hole. Before the glue sets completely, use the metal clamp to arrange the blossom by rolling and repositioning the center.

Photo 1 – Cutting the swirl with decorative edge scissors.

Photo 2 – Twirling the cut swirl around a hemostat (metal clamp).

Photo 3 – A finished, formed rose before gluing.

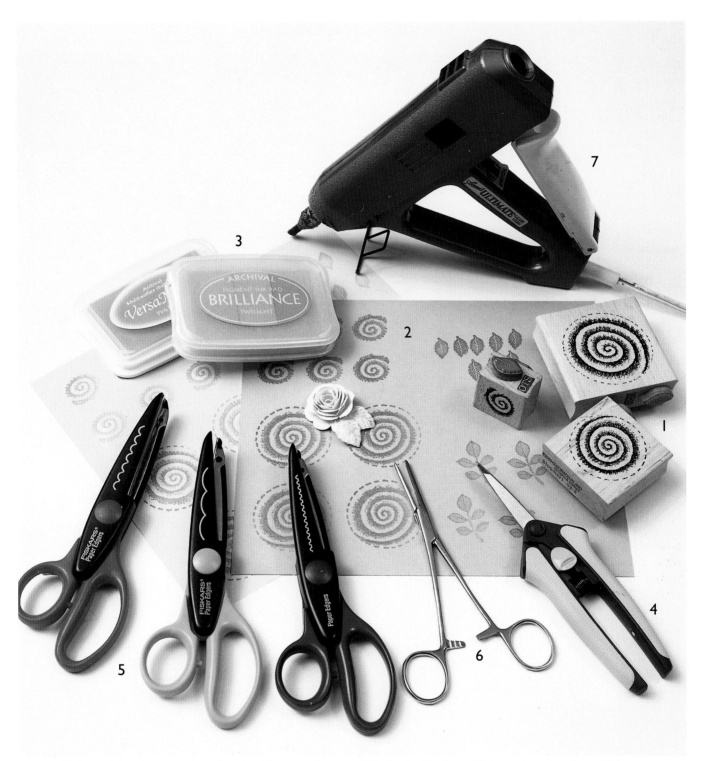

Pictured below: 1) Swirl stamps, 2) card stock with stamped images, 3) inkpads, 4) scissors, 5) decorative edge scissors, 6) hemostat (metal clamp), 7) glue gun with clear glue sticks

Continued from page 20.

Making Swirl Roses: Use plain scallop, large scallop, and pinked scalloped decorative edge scissors for cutting. Use the metal clamp to further shape each petal by grasping and rolling it slightly.

Making Swirl Zinnias:
Cutting the swirl with tiny motif decorative scissors (e.g., tiny scallop, tiny pinking) creates zinnia-type blossoms. After you cut out the swirl, cut a fringe along the edge with straight-blade scissors, using the motifs cut by the decorative edge scissors as a guide, and then roll and form the blossom.

Example A – Zinnia-type blossoms cut with tiny scallop, tiny pinking, and stamp edge decorative scissors, using a variety of paper and ink colors.

Example B – A variety of roses cut with different decorative scissors using a variety of paper and ink colors.

Example C – Two roses showing the variation achieved with one pair of decorative scissors. I used the same large scallop-edge scissors for both roses – one was cut with the rounded scallop up; the other has the pointed edge of the scallop up.

Examples of Swirl Flowers

22

Shaping Paper

Shaped paper pieces add dimension to your quilled designs. You can use stamped cutouts or punched paper pieces to create shaped flowers and foliage.

Basic Supplies & Tools

- Card stock
- Leaf or flower paper punch *or* rubber stamp, inkpad, and scissors
- Embossing pad, such as a thin foam pad or a computer mouse pad
- Paper embosser – A nylon shaping tool, a spoon-shaped embosser, or a large ball metal embosser
- Stamped or punched out paper shapes
- Adhesive – White glue *or* clear hot glue *or* glue dots

Making Shaped Leaves

1. Punch a leaf shape from card stock with a paper punch *or* stamp a leaf design on card stock with a rubber stamp and cut out.
2. Place the paper shape, stamped or colored side down, on the embossing pad.
3. Press the paper embosser into the shape, using a circular motion. (The cut shape will become curved.)
4. Adhere the shape to the surface. I like to use a drop of hot glue – it helps preserve the shape of the paper piece and gives it a raised appearance. Don't use so much glue that it shows on the finished design.

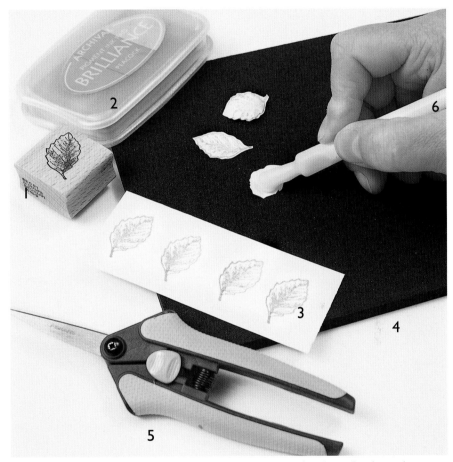

Pictured above: Using an embosser to shape paper pieces. The photo also shows the supplies you need for making shaped paper pieces: 1) rubber stamp with a leaf motif, 2) inkpad, 3) card stock (stamped with leaf images), 4) embossing mat (a thin foam pad or mouse pad), 5) scissors (for cutting out stamped images), 6) embosser (a nylon shaping tool; a spoon-shaped or large ball metal embosser could be used).

Making Shaped Flowers

1. Punch a flower shape from card stock. You could also use a cutout stamped design as well.
2. Place the paper shape, colored side up, on the embossing pad.
3. Press the paper embosser into the middle of the shape until the petals bend upwards. On large flowers, shape each petal individually with the embosser.
4. Adhere the shape to the surface. I like to use a tiny dimensional glue dot to give a raised appearance.

Husking

Husking is an easy paper shaping technique – you loop the paper strips around pins stuck in a corkboard to create a shape and then outline the shape (it's called "hooping") with another paper strip called the collar. Sometimes additional collars are wrapped around pins outside of the first collar to form a larger or different shape.

Designing your own shapes on graph paper is an easy way to create an endless array of shapes. You also can buy an introductory kit to learn this art that consists of husking boards and patterns to get you started. For the husked designs in this book, I have included patterns.

Basic Supplies & Tools

- Quilling paper strips
- Corkboard
- Glass-tipped straight pins
- Husking pattern
- Graph paper – You can download graph paper from the Internet and print it on your computer printer. Most of the designs in this book were done on 3/16" graph paper.
- Black marker
- Wax paper
- White glue

How to

1. Photocopy the patterns in the book or transfer the husking pattern to graph paper. Trim the pattern (if necessary), place it on the corkboard, and cover with a piece of wax paper.
2. Make a tiny (¼") fold at one end of a quilling paper strip. Glue the end to form a loop. (This loop holds the paper strip in place on a pin as you form the shape.) Place a pin in the loop and insert in position #1 on the pattern.
3. Place a pin in position #2. Loop the paper strip around the pin, following the pattern arrow. Bring the strip down to the #1 position and glue to secure. Use the same procedure to loop the paper around all the numbered position points, following the directions of the arrows. Each time you come back to the #1 position, secure the strip with a tiny drop of glue.
4. When you have looped the strip around all the pin positions, wrap a collar around all the outer pins and glue the strips together at each pin. To finish, glue the strip below the #1 position pin and trim off any excess paper.
5. Remove the pins and lift the husked shape. If directed by the pattern, pinch the shape to create different husked designs.

tips: HUSKING

- Keep the paper strips pushed down at the #1 pin to keep the edges even.
- Unlike quilling, use full lengths of quilling paper strips to form the loops and trim off the excess. For larger shapes, glue strips together at the #1 pin and continue looping.
- Insert one pin at a time into the pattern to make it easier to wrap around the other pins.
- Fill in the open spaces in husked shapes with quilled shapes for an even more decorative piece.
- Place two different colored strips together and glue at the end to form a multi-colored husked shape.

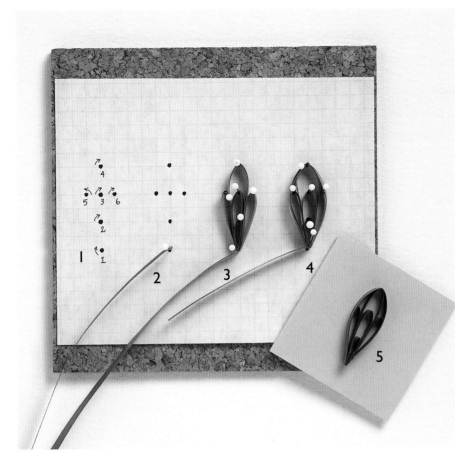

The Basic Steps

Step 1 – The transferred pattern with numbers and arrows marked.

Step 2 – The loop at the end of the quilling strip is placed on a pin in position #1.

Step 3 – The paper strip looped around the pins, following the numbers in sequence and directional arrows.

Step 4 – Making the collar around the design.

Step 5 – The finished piece.

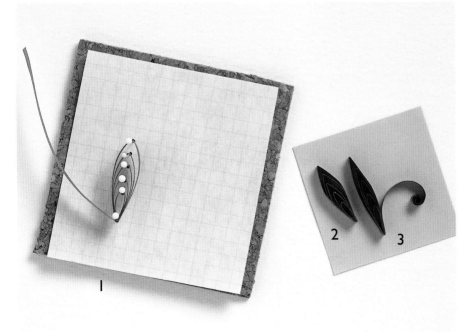

Basic Wheatear

The wheatear shape is formed by looping a paper strip around pins in a straight line. You can vary the shape by placing the pins closer together or farther apart, and you can pinch and curve the wheatear to form other shapes. To make a wheatear with a scroll, do not trim the end of the paper strip; instead, curl it with a quilling tool to create a single scroll.

The photo at left shows (1) a basic wheatear shape with pins, (2) a wheatear with the top pinched to a point, and (3) a wheatear with a scroll.

Coloring Paper

Learning to color your own quilling strips and paper panels gives you a wider variety of paper colors to work with and allows you to make customized pieces by blending colors. I use stamp pad ink for coloring. I especially love the stamp pads with lots of sections in different colors because they provide a large palette to work from. There are many different brushes and applicators available for coloring your paper with inkpads, but I prefer a stencil brush – it's the easiest way to apply smooth, even color. You will need at least four stencil brushes: one for reds and oranges, one for greens, one for blues and purples, and one for white and metallic colors. You do not need to wash the brushes between uses; the bristles will stay soft.

Basic Supplies & Tools
- Quilling paper, ⅜" wide
- Inkpad with regular ink or pigment ink
- Stencil brush, one for each color group, ½" to 1"
- Paper towels

How to
1. Tap the stencil brush on the surface of the inkpad to load it with color.
2. Rub the color on the paper, using a circular scrubbing motion. Your goal is a smooth, even layer of color.
   - To make the color darker, keep adding layers of ink until you are pleased with the results.
   - If your coloring is uneven, try using a larger brush.
   - To remove excess color from the brush – if you're moving from a light blue to a dark purple, for example – rub the brush on a pile of dry paper towels.

Pictured above left: Supplies and tools for coloring include (top to bottom) a paper punch, a stamp pad, paper towels, a stencil brush.
Pictured above right: 1) a white paper strip shaded dark blue to white, 2) a punched, colored paper strip, and 3) finished punched flowers.

Coloring Fringed Flowers
Color ⅜" wide quilling paper before fringing to create a shaded fringed flower.

Pictured right, top to bottom: Shaded and colored quilling paper, the finished fringed flower.

This paper strip was shaded with two colors of ink and punched to create the flowers.

The steps for creating a colored swirl flower.

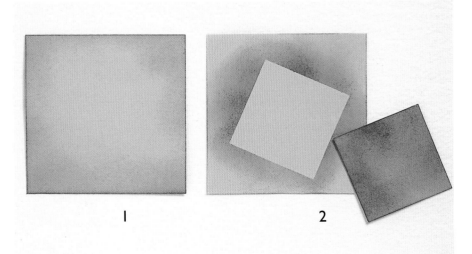

Pictured left to right: A paper panel with shaded edges, paper colored around a masking panel.

Coloring Punched Flowers

1. With a paper trimmer, cut a 1½" strip of white paper.
2. Starting on one end, color the strip shading to white on the other end or blend two different colors for a gorgeous result.
3. Punch out the flowers, shape them, and glue to the project in order from dark to light.

Coloring Swirl Flowers

You can create a wide variety of shaded roses by coloring the paper before cutting and rolling. The spiral is stamped on the back of the paper and used as a pattern only; the flower is made with the colored side of the paper facing up.

1. Stamp the spiral on a piece of card stock. Trim the paper close to the stamped shape.
2. Turn over the paper and apply color to make a shaded comma shape. Cut out the swirl with decorative edge scissors.
3. Roll the swirl with the colored side on the inside so it's visible in the finished flower.

Coloring Paper Panels

Coloring the edge of a paper panel or folded card is a favorite way to frame a design. Here are two examples: colored paper with shaded edges and colored masked shapes.

Shaded Edges: Place the paper on a protected work surface and color the edges with the inkpad and stencil brush.

Masked Shapes: Create shapes with a masking panel or a stencil cut from paper.

1. Affix the shape or stencil in place with low-tack tape or a very small piece of double-sided tape.
2. Apply color around the shape, concentrating on the edges.
3. Remove the masking panel or stencil to reveal the shape.

Card Art

Greeting cards are the most popular base for quilled designs. In this section, I share some favorite techniques for creating cards and envelopes. I hope this large array of card and tag projects will inspire you to make personalized greeting cards for your friends.

Making Card Bases

You can readily buy pre-folded card blanks, but it's easier and more economical to simply cut and fold your own. Using basic tools and techniques, it's also easy to cut a window (or windows) in a card. Cutout windows make nice frames for the small paper sculptures created with quilling.

Basic Supplies & Tools

- Card stock, 8½" x 11"
- Paper trimmer
- Bone folder
- Craft knife
- Metal cork-backed ruler
- Self-healing cutting mat
- Pencil
- White or art gum eraser
- Liner paper and double-sided tape
- *Optional:* Shape cutter and templates (for cutting round, oval, and shaped windows)

How to

Make the Card:

This size card fits into a standard size A-2 invitation envelope, which is 5¾" x 4⅜". Feel free to customize the size and shape of your card blank.

1. Cut the card stock in half to make two pieces, each 5½" x 8½".
2. Fold the paper in half to make a folded card blank 5½" x 4¼". Use the bone folder to make a sharp, even fold. (Photo 1)

Cut a Square or Rectangular Window:

1. On the inside left side of the card, measure and lightly mark out the window(s). (Photo 2)
2. Place the card on a cutting mat and use a paper trimmer or craft knife to cut out the window(s). (Photo 3) (You can use the cutout as a panel

Photo 1 – Folding a card.

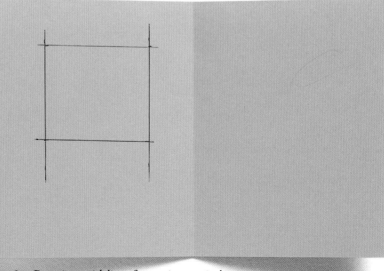

Photo 2 – Drawing guidelines for cutting a window.

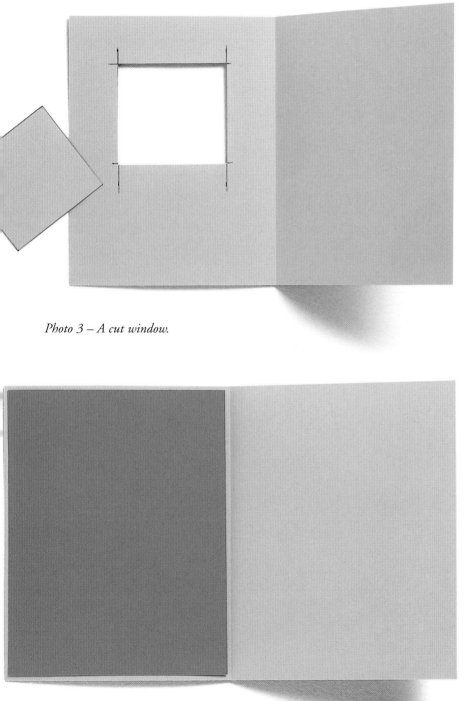

Photo 3 – A cut window.

Photo 4 – A paper liner covers the inside left panel of the card.

Pictured at right: "Photo Card." See page 86 for instructions.

on the envelope or as an accent inside the card.)

3. Carefully erase the pencil marks.

Cut a Shaped Window:

1. Measure and mark the placement of the window.
2. Use the template and shape cutter to cut out the window. (You can use the cutout as a panel on the envelope or as an accent inside the card.)
3. Carefully erase any visible marks.

Make a Liner:

1. Cut either a paper panel slightly smaller than the card front. (It needs to be smaller to ensure the fold is not covered.)
2. Attach the liner panel with double-sided tape along all the edges. (Photo 4) Make sure the tape does not show through the window.

Folded Liner Option: Open the card. Cut a piece of lining paper slightly smaller on all sides than the open card. Fold in half. Use double-sided tape along the fold to adhere the liner inside the card.

Making Your Own Envelopes

It's easy to create your own decorative envelopes for cards. You can buy envelope templates or try this method, which uses recycled envelopes as templates. Simply collect envelopes in a variety of sizes and shapes to make different templates. Look for ones with a variety of flap shapes, too.

Use your envelopes for mailing custom card shapes and sizes. Envelopes are a great way to recycle any piece of paper that's slightly larger than the envelope template. Try wrapping paper, an interesting page from a magazine, a picture from a calendar, or a scrap of decorative paper.

Basic Supplies & Tools

- Paper
- A previously used envelope that fits your card (to use as a template)
- Bone folder
- Scissors
- Glue stick
- Decorative labels

How to

1. Carefully take apart the used envelope and lay it flat. If you rip a portion, repair it with clear tape.
2. Using a small piece of double-sided tape, place the envelope template on the wrong side of the paper. (Photo 1)
3. Fold up each side of the paper, using the template as a guide, and crease with the bone folder.
4. With the scissors, trim around the template and remove the excess paper. Remove the template.

5. Using a glue stick, assemble the envelope. (Photo 2)

6. Place a label in the front for the address. See the finished envelopes in the photo for an example.

Photo 1 – The template is positioned on the wrong side of the envelope paper.

Photo 2 – The back of the assembled envelope.

Lining Envelopes

This is a very quick, easy way to add elegance to a simple envelope with a paper lining to match your handmade card. You can make the lining from a paper you used in your card design or a piece of coordinating wrapping paper. The method works for all sizes and types of envelopes.

Basic Supplies & Tools
- Envelope
- Decorative paper, for lining
- Scissors
- Glue stick
- Bone folder

Photo 1 – Cutting the top shape to fit the envelope flap.

Continued on next page.

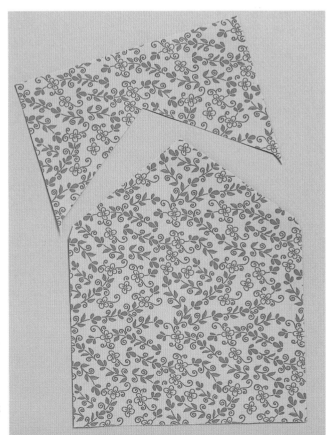

Lining envelopes, continued from page 33.

How to

1. Cut the decorative paper the width of the envelope and the height of the envelope with the flap up.
2. Place the decorative paper piece in the envelope. To make the liner, cut the decorative paper around the shape of the flap. (Photo 1)
3. Remove the liner from the envelope. Trim ⅜" off the bottom. Place the paper liner back in the envelope. (The glue strip on the envelope will be exposed.) (Photo 2)
4. Lift the liner and rub a glue stick along the envelope flap just below the glue strip. Press the liner over the glue and rub to adhere. (Photo 3)

Photo 2 – Liner is cut to size of envelope. The bottom will be trimmed.

Photo 3 – Trimmed liner inserted into envelope.

5. Fold down the flap and crease the fold with the bone folder. Your lined envelope is ready to use.

Pictured at left: Finished lined envelopes.

Lettering

There are a number of ways to add verbal greetings and sentiments to cards. The photo below shows a variety of examples.

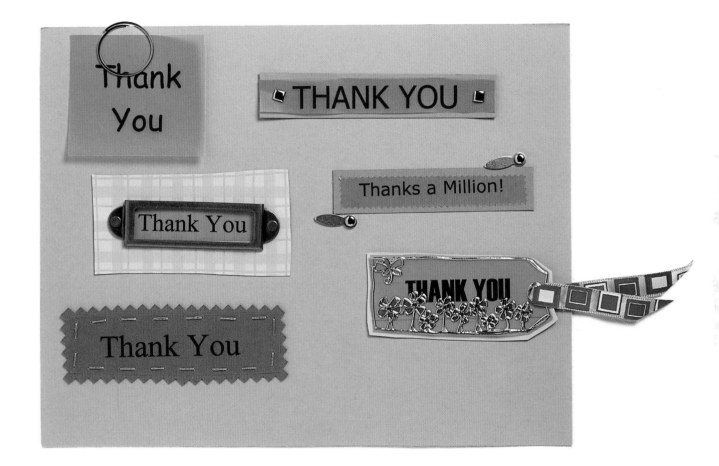

- **Stickers and transfers.** You'll find an amazing selection of clear-back stickers and rub-on transfers to add a word or phrase to your card.
- **Rubber stamps.** Having a rubber stamp alphabet and an inkpad handy makes it easy to add words to your card creations.
- **Handwriting.** Add a greeting in your own handwriting (the best technique) with a colored gel pen, a fine-tip marker, or calligraphy pen.
- **Computer printing.** Using your computer is a great way to create a customized greeting on a card. Use a variety of fonts and ink colors to print words and sayings on colored card stock or vellum sheets. TIPS: Print a full sheet with a variety of sentiments ready to cut and use. Add a box frame around the lettering in very light gray ink for easy cutting.

Pictured above: A full sheet of "thank you" printed on a vellum sheet. This sample shows a number of ways to attach and use on your card creations. The sheet is printed with black ink, but you can have even more variety with decorative fonts printed in color.

Gift Tags

Gift tags are the simplest cards to make – no folding or envelopes required. You can cut your own tags from card stock or purchase ready-made tags for decorating. When you're creating a quilled card, use any leftover pieces – fringed flowers, quilled shapes, or sculptured paper pieces – to create a gift tag. Loop ribbons, string, or lengths of trim through the hole and attach them to boxes, wrapped packages, and gift bags.

Pictured above: A gift tag on a wrapped package.

Pictured at right: A quilled card adds the finishing touch to a gift jar.

I Got You Babe!

Colorful letter stickers, quilled hearts, and computer generated
lettering are combined to make a bright, modern card.

SUPPLIES

Base:

White card blank, 5½" x 4¼"
(folded size)

Papers:

Olive green card stock, 5" x 3½"

Quilling strips, ⅛" – Pink, yellow,
purple, light blue

Large alphabet stickers to spell
"Babe"

White card stock

Envelope to fit card

Tools & Other Supplies:

Basic supplies and tools for quilling

Double-sided tape

Scissors

Craft knife

Cutting mat

Computer and printer

tip:

When you're using a computer
to create lettering, fomat four
panels to a page with different
sayings to economize on paper.

INSTRUCTIONS

Make the Quilled Elements:

See the beginning of the book for detailed instructions.

1. Heart shape – (Make 7.) Using all the colors, tear the quilling strips into 3"
   and 4" lengths. Make scrolled hearts.
2. Peg (for dimension) – (Make 12.) Cut 4" lengths of ⅛" quilling strips of
   any color. For each letter sticker, make three tight coils.

Decorate & Assemble:

1. Using the photo as a guide, generate lettering on the olive green card stock
   with a computer and printer.
2. Mount the panel to the card front with double-sided tape.
3. Place the letter stickers to form "Babe" in order on a piece of white card
   stock. Trim around the entire word, leaving a ⅛" border around all the letters.
4. With the white glue, glue the tight coils to the backs of the letters. Glue the
   letters in place on the card front.
5. Use white glue to adhere the quilled hearts on the front of the card. ❑

Kisses & Hugs Card

This colorful card is quickly fashioned with letter stickers and quilled hearts. Stamped sentiments provide a personal touch.

SUPPLIES

Base:

Pink card blank, 5½" x 4-¼" (folded size)

Papers:

Olive green card stock, 5" x 3¾"

Quilling strips, ⅛" – Pink, yellow, purple, light blue

Large alphabet stickers – 2 Xs, 2 Os

White card stock

Envelope to fit card

Tools & Other Supplies:

Basic supplies and tools for quilling

Double-sided tape

Scissors

Craft knife

Cutting mat

Alphabet rubber stamps

Ink pad

INSTRUCTIONS

Make the Quilled Elements:

See the beginning of the book for detailed instructions.

1. Heart shape – (Make 6.) Using all the colors, tear the quilling strips into 3" and 4" lengths. Make scrolled hearts.
2. Peg (for dimension) – (Make 6.) Cut 4" lengths of ⅛" quilling strips of any color. For each X sticker, make three tight coils.

Decorate & Assemble:

1. Using the photo as a guide, stamp "Kiss!" and "Hug!" on the olive green card stock.
2. Mount the panel to the card front with double-sided tape.
3. Place the X and O stickers on white card stock. Trim around each letter, leaving a ⅛" border around each one. Cut away the inside sections of letters, using a craft knife and cutting mat.
4. With the white glue, glue the tight coils to the backs of the Xs. Glue the Os, then the Xs in place on the card front.
5. Use white glue to adhere the quilled hearts on the front of the card. ❏

Make A Wish Card

Blow out the candles and make a wish!

SUPPLIES

Base:

Light blue card blank, 5½" x 4¼"
   (folded size)

Papers:

Quilling strips, ⅛" – Orange,
   yellow, black, light gray

Quilling strips, ⅜" – Yellow

Envelope

Tools & Other Supplies:

Basic supplies and tools for quilling

Rub-on lettering *or* computer and
   printer

Light blue inkpad

Stencil brush

Dimensional glue dots

Double-sided tape

INSTRUCTIONS

Make the Quilled Elements:

See the beginning of the book for detailed instructions.

1. Flame – (Make 4.) Glue together orange and yellow ⅛" strips. Tear into 4" lengths. Make eccentric multicolor petal shapes. Curl the tips of the flames slightly.
2. Smoke – (Make 3.) Cut 1" to 2" lengths of light gray paper strips. Make them into single scrolls.
3. Wick – (Make 5.) Cut ¼" to ½" pieces from ⅛" black paper strips.
4. Candle – (Make 5.) Cut ⅜" yellow paper strips into 1¾" to 2½" pieces. Cut the top of each piece at an angle.

Decorate & Assemble:

1. Add the rub-on or computer generated lettering to the card front.
2. With the inkpad and stencil brush, color each candle piece and the edges of the card front to soften the lettering.
3. Arrange the candles on the card front, using the photo as a guide. Attach with dimensional glue dots.
4. Using the photo as a guide, glue the quilled elements to the card. ❑

Dandelion Wish Card

Punched shapes from decorative paper and quilled pieces
are put together for this contemporary design.

SUPPLIES

Base:

Light blue card blank, 5" x 7"
(folded size)

Papers:

Quilling strips, ⅛" – Purple, white

Blue patterned paper panel,
3¾" x 6¼"

Blue polka dot card stock

Light purple card stock

Envelope

Tools & Other Supplies:

Basic supplies and tools for quilling

Purple gel pen

Decorative punches – Starburst,
2½" and 1¼"

Round punch, ⅜"

Double-sided tape

Glue stick

INSTRUCTIONS

Make the Quilled Elements:

See the beginning of the book for detailed instructions.

1. Seed – (Make 6.) Tear 5" pieces of purple quilling paper. Crease each 5" length at 3". Quill to the fold and make a teardrop shape. Fold the remaining 2" in half and glue.
2. Seed fluff – (Make 6.) Accordion fold white quilling strips at ⅜" intervals, making four folds. Glue the purple seed piece into the middle fold. Glue folds together.
3. Peg (for dimension) – (Make 4.) Tear 4" lengths of ⅛" light purple quilling paper. Make tight coils.

Decorate & Assemble:

1. Using double-sided tape, adhere the blue patterned paper panel to the card front.
2. To make the dandelion petals, punch one 2½" starburst shape each from polka dot and light purple card stock. Punch one 1¼" starburst shape from polka dot card stock for a flower center. Punch one round shape from light purple card stock for the other flower center.
3. Cut ¼" wide strips of the card stocks for flower stems.
4. Glue flower petals and stems in place, using the glue stick.
5. With the white glue, glue the tight coils to the backs of the flower centers. Glue in place on the card front.
6. Glue the quilled shapes in place, tucking some under the raised punched shapes.
7. Write "Make a wish" under the panel with the gel pen. ❑

41

Ice Cream Cone Cards

Just a few simple coils piled on top of each other give the look of a yummy treat!
Change the quilling paper colors to change the flavor of your ice cream.

SUPPLIES

Bases:

Light pink card blank, 4¼" x 6"
 (folded size)

Light green card blank, 4¼" x 6"
 (folded size)

Papers:

Quilling strips, ⅛" – Brown/white
 variegated (for chocolate),
 pink/white variegated (for
 strawberry)

2 panels of pink polka dot paper,
 each 4⅛" x 5⅞" (folded size, for
 liners)

Tan card stock (for the cones)

Envelopes to fit cards

Tools & Other Supplies:

Basic supplies and tools for quilling

Black marker

Double-sided tape

Optional: Diamond texture plate,
 embossing tool

INSTRUCTIONS

Make the Quilled Elements:

See the beginning of the book for detailed instructions.

Scoop of Ice Cream – (Make 8 or 9 for each card.) Cut 2" and 4" lengths (for a variety of sizes) of ⅛" quilling strips. Shape into loose coils. Shape one into a teardrop shape for the melting scoop of ice cream.

Decorate & Assemble:

1. Cut 2" square windows in the front panels of the cards. See "Making

Card Bases."

2. Tape the liner paper in place. See the "Folded Liner Option" with "Making Card Bases."

3. Add lettering to the card front, e.g., "Here's the scoop... Happy Birthday!" or "Take life one scoop at a time...it's delicious!"

4. Create the cone by cutting out a 1¼" long triangle from the tan paper.

5. Glue the cone into the window on the liner paper.

6. Add the ice cream scoops and dripping scoop, layering the coils to create dimension. ❏

Take Life one Scoop at a Time...

...it's delicious!

Paisley Card & Tag

The chipboard letter on the card front can be the initial of the card recipient's name or the first letter of a sentiment such as "thank you" that is written on the inside of the card. This project also includes a matching gift tag.

SUPPLIES

Base:

Brown card blank, 4½" x 6" (folded size)

Papers:

Quilling strips, ⅛" – Brown, blue, white, brown/white variegated and shaded, blue/white variegated

Green and blue paisley paper panel, 4¼" x 5¾"

Distressed blue paper panel, 2" x 5½"

White card stock

Envelope

Tools & Other Supplies:

Basic supplies and tools for quilling

Decorative edge scissors – Mini pinking

Chipboard letter

Sandpaper

Glue dots, dimensional

Double-sided tape

For the tag: Hole punch, eyelet, ⅓ yd. *each* two types of decorative fibers in coordinating colors

INSTRUCTIONS

Make the Quilled Elements:

See the beginning of the book for detailed instructions. I varied the colors on the different parts of the large paisley shape – use any of the browns or blues.

1. Large paisley – (Make 4.) Using blue or brown quilling strips, tear an 11" length and make an eccentric coil. Pinch at the glued edge into a petal shape. Glue each shape on a piece of white card stock. Trim around the shapes with mini pinking scissors.
2. Two-toned small paisley – (Make 4.) Glue a 2" blue and 2" white quilling strip together. Coil from the blue end to make a petal shape.
3. Small paisley – (Make 7.) Tear 3" lengths of white quilling strips and make into petal shapes.
4. Scroll – (Make 4.) Crimp 6" lengths of brown or blue quilling strips to make V-scrolls.

Decorate & Assemble the Card:

1. With the double-sided tape, adhere the paisley patterned paper panel to the card front.
2. Attach the distressed blue paper panel along the left side of the card front.
3. With the white glue, adhere a piece of distressed blue paper on the chipboard letter. Let dry. Use sandpaper to remove the excess paper and distress the edges.
4. Glue three large paisley shapes to the blue panel, using the photo as a guide. Using the photo as a guide, adhere three two-tone small paisley shapes and six small paisley shapes around the large paisley shapes.
5. Using dimensional glue dots, place the chipboard letter.

Decorate & Assemble the Tag:

1. Cut a 2½" x 4½" green paisley card panel. Trim the top corners to create tag shape.
2. Glue to dark brown card. Trim around the tag shape, leaving a ⅛" frame.
3. Glue a 2¼" square of blue distressed paper on the tag.
4. Glue the remaining quilled paisley shapes on the distressed paper.
5. Add an eyelet at the top of the tag. Thread with 12" lengths of brown and blue decorative fibers. ❏

Initial Place Cards

Chipboard letters are easy to find and ready to use for these delightful place cards. You could also make initial cards without the computer-generated names and line them up to spell a name as a mantel or table decoration for a birthday party or other celebration.

SUPPLIES

Base:

Green and bright blue card blank, 1¾" x 4" (folded size)

Papers:

Quilling strips, ⅛" – Light green, olive green, bright green

Light blue paper panel, printed with computer-generated name and trimmed to 1¾" x various heights (depending on name)

Card stock – Bright green, bright blue

Tools & Other Supplies:

Basic supplies and tools for quilling

Chipboard letters (one for each card)

Double-sided tape

Scissors

Craft knife

Cutting mat

INSTRUCTIONS

Make the Quilled Elements:

See the beginning of the book for detailed instructions.

1. Leaf – (Make 3 per card.) Tear papers into 4" lengths. Make leaf shapes.
2. Scroll – (Make 4 per card.) Cut papers into 2" to 3" lengths. Make single scrolls.
3. Peg (for dimension) – (Make 3 or 4 per letter.) Cut 4" lengths of light green paper. Make tight coils.

Decorate & Assemble:

1. Glue the chipboard letter on green or blue paper. Let dry.
2. Trim away the excess paper, leaving a ⅛" border. Use a craft knife and cutting mat to cut away inside areas.
3. With a glue stick, glue the light blue paper panels with printed names on green or blue paper. Trim, leaving a ⅛" border at top and bottom.
4. Glue the name panels near the bottoms of the folded cards.
5. With white glue, glue the tight coils to the backs of the chipboard letters. Glue the letters in place on the card fronts.
6. With the white glue, add the quilled pieces to the cards. Combine the various green colors in different ways for variety. ❏

Hold a Friend Accordion Card

This accordion-folded card has a quote on the cover that's surrounded with quilled shapes. You can change the colors of the quilling strips to match a favorite quote.

SUPPLIES

Base:
Accordion book, 3" square

Papers:
Quilling strips, ⅛" – Dark green

Sticker quote *or* computer generated quote

Paper images or lettering (for decorating inside pages)

Card stock (if using a sticker quote)

Tools & Other Supplies:
Basic supplies and tools for quilling
Scissors

INSTRUCTIONS

Make the Quilled Elements:
See the beginning of the book for detailed instructions.

1. Scroll – (Make 4.) Cut strips into 4" lengths. Make an S-scroll for each corner

2. Leaf – (Make 18 to 20.) Tear strips into 3" to 4" lengths for a variety of sizes. Make leaf shapes.

3. Peg (for dimension) – (Make 5.) Cut 6" lengths of any color. Make tight coils.

Decorate & Assemble:

1. Decorate the inside with paper images or lettering.

2. **If you're using a sticker quote,** place the sticker on a piece of

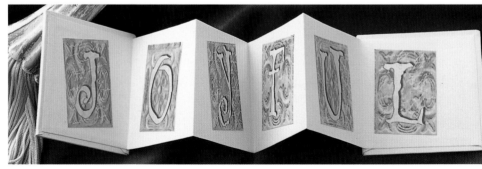

matching card stock. Trim.

3. With white glue, glue the tight coils to the back of the quote. Glue to the center of the front.

4. With white glue, add the quilled

pieces, using the photo as a guide. Tuck some pieces under the raised quote and some over the top of the quote to add dimension. ❏

Dare to Dream Accordion Card

Accent a favorite quote with a colorful quilled flower and leaves and decorate the cover of an accordion-folded book to make a unique gift card. Change the colors of the quilling strips to match your quote.

SUPPLIES

Base:

Accordion book, 3" square

Papers:

Quilling strips, ⅛" – Yellow, red, black

Sticker quote *or* computer generated quote

Paper images or lettering (for decorating inside pages)

Card stock (if using a sticker quote)

Tools & Other Supplies:

Basic supplies and tools for quilling

Scissors

INSTRUCTIONS

Make the Quilled Elements:

See the beginning of the book for detailed instructions.

1. Red dot – (Make 8.) Tear 2", 3", and 4" lengths red quilling strips for a variety of sizes. Make tight coils.
2. Flower – (Make 13.) Tear 4" lengths of yellow quilling strips. Make petal shapes.
3. Scroll – (Make 7 or 8.) Cut 2" to 3" lengths of black. Make single scrolls.
4. Peg (for dimension) – (Make 5.) Cut 6" lengths of any color. Make tight coils.

Decorate & Assemble:

1. Decorate the inside with paper images or lettering.
2. **If you're using a sticker quote,** place the sticker on a piece of

matching card stock. Trim.
3. With white glue, glue the tight coils to the back of the quote. Glue to front, placing the quote just slightly off center.
4. With white glue, arrange the quilled

pieces around the quote, using the photo as a guide. Tuck some flower petals and scroll pieces under the raised quote. Place some petals over the top of the quote to add dimension. ❑

Eiffel Tower Card

Quilling and husking techniques are combined to create a likeness
of the Eiffel Tower on a card with a decided French flair.

SUPPLIES

Base:

Olive green card blank, 6" x 4¼"
    (folded size)

Papers:

Quilling strips, ⅛" – Black

Sage green card stock, 1½" x 4¼"
    (panel for quilled image)

Old postcard image, 5¼" x 3¼"

French postage stamp

Stickers and collage images

Old letter

Brown diamond patterned paper
    (for the envelope)

Label (for the envelope)

Tools & Other Supplies:

Basic supplies and tools for quilling

Basic supplies and tools for husking
    (See "Husking.")

Brown inkpad

Stencil brush

4 copper brads

Glue stick

Scissors

INSTRUCTIONS

Make the Husked Elements:

See "Husking" for detailed instructions.

1. Using ⅛" black quilling paper and the patterns provided, make one top
   tower piece and two bottom tower pieces.

2. Pinch the bottom tower pieces to create the flat bottoms.

Make the Quilled Elements:

See the beginning of the book for detailed instructions.

1. Tower cross piece – (Make 3 in all.) Tear two 5" lengths of black paper and
   one 7" length. Make diamonds.

2. Tower top – (Make 1.) Tear a 1½" length of paper and make a tight coil.

Decorate & Assemble:

1. Color the edges of the sage green panel for the quilled image with brown
   ink, using a stencil brush.

2. Crumple the old letter, smooth, and color with brown ink, using a stencil
   brush.

PATTERN

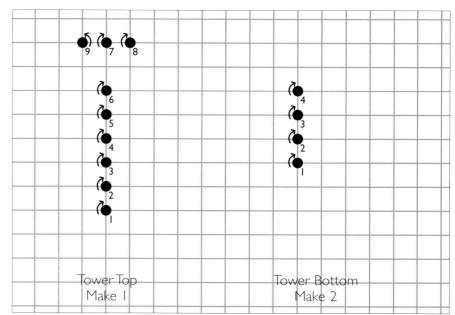

Tower Top
Make 1

Tower Bottom
Make 2

3. Arrange the collage elements on the card, using the photo as a guide. Start with the larger pieces, then accent with the stamp, stickers, and cut images.

4. Attach the sage green panel to the right side of the card with four brads.

5. Glue the tower pieces to the sage green panel.

Make the Envelope:

1. Make an envelope from brown diamond paper. (See "Making Your Own Envelopes.")

2. Add a label on the front for the address. ❑

Lavender Collage Card

Paper pieces with a vintage look and a quilled motif are combined to make this collage on a card.

SUPPLIES

Base:

Olive or sage green card blank, 6" x 4¼" (folded size)

Papers:

Quilling strips, ⅛" – Dark purple, light purple, blue, dark green

Sage green card stock, 1½" x 4¼" (panel for quilled image)

Old postcard image, 5¼" x 3¼"

French postage stamp

Stickers and collage images

Old letter

Brown diamond patterned paper (for the envelope)

Label (for the envelope)

Tools & Other Supplies:

Basic supplies and tools for quilling

Brown inkpad

Stencil brush

4 copper brads

Glue stick

Scissors

INSTRUCTIONS

Make the Quilled Elements:

See the beginning of the book for detailed instructions.

1. Curly Lavender Flower – (Make 13 shapes in all.) Tear thirteen 3" to 4" lengths of purple and blue quilling strips. Make four tight coils and nine teardrop shapes.
2. Leaf – (Make 3.) Tear 4" lengths of dark green quilling paper. Make leaf shapes.
3. Stem – (Make 1.) Cut 4" of dark green quilling paper. Quill the top 1½", glue the tail, and form into a teardrop shape.
4. Scroll – (Make 2.) Cut 2" lengths of dark green quilling paper. Make single scrolls.

Decorate & Assemble:

1. Color the edges of the sage green panel for the quilled image with brown ink, using a stencil brush.
2. Crumple the old letter, smooth, and color with brown ink, using a stencil brush.
3. Arrange the collage elements on the card, using the photo as a guide. Start with the larger pieces, then accent with the stamp, stickers, and cut images.
4. Attach the sage green panel to the right side of the card with four brads.
5. Arrange the quilled pieces, using the photo as a guide, and glue to the sage green panel.

Make the Envelope:

1. Make an envelope from brown diamond paper. (See "Making Your Own Envelopes.")
2. Add a label on the front for the address. ❑

Thank You Daisy Card

The daisy patterned paper and quilled daisy are a lovely way to say "Thank you."

SUPPLIES

Base:

Pale yellow card blank, 5½" x 4¼" (folded size)

Papers:

Quilling strips, ⅛" – Yellow, yellow/white variegated, green

Pale yellow panel, 1¾" x 4¼"

Daisy patterned paper panel, 5¼" x 4"

Vellum with computer-generated "thank you"

Envelope

Tools & Other Supplies:

Basic supplies and tools for quilling

Basic supplies and tools for husking

2 square gold brads

Scissors

Glue stick

½ yd. decorative yellow fibers

INSTRUCTIONS

Make the Quilled Elements:

See the beginning of the book for detailed instructions.

1. Daisy petal – (Make 8.) Tear 5" pieces of yellow/white variegated quilling strips. Make into eccentric coils, then into eye shapes.
2. Daisy center – (Make 1.) Tear a 5" yellow quilling strip. Make into one tight coil.

Make the Husked Elements:

See "Husking" for detailed instructions.

Leaves – (Make 2, one with a scroll.) Using green quilling paper, make husking wheatears with three loops spaced ⅜" apart.

Decorate & Assemble:

1. Using a glue stick, attach the daisy patterned panel and the yellow panel to the card front.
2. Attach the computer generated vellum strip to the card with the brads.
3. Using the photo as a guide, arrange the quilled pieces to make the daisy. Glue on the card.
4. Tie the decorative fibers around the top of the card. ❑

Thanks A Latte!

Just a few quilled scrolls accent this caffeine-induced creation!

SUPPLIES

Base:

Dark brown card blank, 5½" square (folded size)

Papers:

Quilling strips, ⅛" – Light tan

Tan paper panel, 4¾" square

Tan and cream patterned paper

Decorative newspaper paper

Tan paper panel, 3" x ½", with computer generated "thanks a latte!"

Tools & Other Supplies:

Basic supplies and tools for quilling

Basic supplies and tools for making swirl flowers

Inkpads – Black, brown, gold

Stencil brushes

Gold watercolor paint and applicator

4 copper brads

½ yd. decorative braid

Decorative edge scissors – Scallop

Instant coffee

Coffee cup

Sponge

INSTRUCTIONS

Make the Quilled Elements:

See the beginning of the book for detailed instructions.

Scrolls – (Make 6.) Cut 1½" to 3" lengths of light tan quilling strips. Make single scrolls.

Make the Swirl Flower:

See "Making Swirl Flowers" for detailed instructions.

1. Stamp the swirl flower on the back of the decorative newspaper paper.
2. Color the front side of the paper with brown ink.
3. Cut out the flower with scallop decorative edge scissors.
4. Form into a zinnia blossom.

Assemble:

1. Make a coffee stain by mixing 1 tablespoon of instant coffee with ½ cup hot water. Sponge and drip the coffee on the square tan panel. Dip the bottom of a cup in the coffee stain and press repeatedly on the paper. Let dry completely.
2. Using the cup pattern provided, cut a shape from tan and cream patterned paper.
3. Shade the edges of the cup with black and brown inks, using a stencil brush.
4. Cut out the masking panel pattern from a scrap of card stock. Shade the top area of the cup, using black and brown inks.
5. Color the "Thanks a latte!" paper panel with brown ink.
6. Color the edges of the front of the card with gold ink.
7. Use double-sided tape to affix the paper panels and coffee cup to the card.
8. Using the photo as a guide, glue the quilled scrolls to the card.
9. Brush the top edges of the scrolls with gold watercolor paint.
10. Loop the braid around the fold of the card as shown. Glue the swirl flower to the braid, letting the ends hang free. ❑

PATTERNS
(actual size)

Masking Panel

Thanks a latte!

Lily of The Valley Card

This card design, inspired by the graceful lines of Art Nouveau, has quilled pieces accented with tiny pearls.

SUPPLIES

Base:

White card blank, 5½" x 4¼"
  (folded size)

Papers:

Quilling strips, ⅛" – White,
  green/white variegated

Light purple card stock, 5¼" x 4"

Light purple patterned paper panel,
  4¾" x 3¼"

Pale blue paper panel, 4¾" x 1¾"

Patterned vellum (for envelope)

Label (for envelope)

Tools & Other Supplies:

Basic supplies and tools for quilling

21 small pearl beads

Scissors

Glue stick

About Lily of the Valley

Lily of the valley is a shade-loving herbaceous perennial plant native to Europe and Northern Asia. It has broad green ribbed leaves and fragrant white bell-shaped flowers with scalloped edges that grow on curved stems. Its botanical name is *Convallaria majalis.*

Traditionally sold on the streets of France on May 1, its French name is *muget de bois.* It is also called May Lily, Ladder-to-Heaven, and Our Lady's Tears (because legend has it that where the tears Mary cried at the crucifixion fell on the ground, lilies of the valley grew). In 1982, lily of the valley became the national flower of Finland.

Its flowers are used to make perfume, and the plant has a history of use in herbal medicine as a tonic to strengthen the heart. In parts of Germany, a wine is prepared from the flowers and mixed with raisins.

Throughout the ages, symbolic meanings originating from folk legends and sacred traditions have been assigned to various plants. In Victorian times, friends and lovers used the meanings of flowers to send a special message in the form of a tussie-mussie or a pressed flower tucked in a card or gift. In the language of flowers, lily of the valley symbolizes sweetness and a return of happiness.

INSTRUCTIONS

Make the Quilled Elements:

See the beginning of the book for detailed instructions.

1. Flower – (Make 9 in all.) Tear ⅛" white quilling strips in 5", 4", and 3" lengths. Make three half moon shapes of varying sizes for each stem.

2. Stalk – (Make 3.) Cut ⅛" light green/white variegated into 3" lengths. Scissor curl to make the stems.

3. Leaf – (Make 3.) For each leaf, tear four 3" pieces from ⅛" light green/white variegated paper. Form harp shapes, each with a small scroll at the top.

4. Scroll – (Make 3.) Cut ⅛" light green/white variegated into 2" lengths. Make single scrolls.

Decorate & Assemble:

1. Using a glue stick, attach the paper panels to the front of the card.

2. Using the photo as a guide, arrange the quilled shapes to form three lilies of the valley. Glue in this order: the harp-shaped leaf, the stalk, and then the scroll. Glue the flowers under the stem with smallest blossom at the end.

3. Using white glue, glue the pearls under the blossoms.

Make the Envelope:

1. Make an envelope from patterned vellum. (See "Making Your Own Envelopes.")

2. Add a label on the front for the address. ❑

Lily of The Valley Tag

By adding elements, changing the leaf color, and using rhinestones, you can easily vary the lily of the valley design. Use this example as a guide for creating variations to other quilled designs.

SUPPLIES

Papers:

Quilling strips, ⅛" – White, teal/white variegated

Light purple patterned paper, 3¼" x 5¼"

Purple card stock

Pale blue paper panel, 3" square

Tools & Other Supplies:

Basic supplies and tools for quilling

3 silver eyelets

3 different light teal and purple decorative fibers, each 10" long

Rhinestone stickers in swirl pattern

Single rhinestones

Scissors

Glue stick

INSTRUCTIONS

Make the Quilled Elements:

See the beginning of the book for detailed instructions.

1. Flower – (Make 6.) Tear ⅛" white quilling strips into 5", 4" and 3" lengths. Make half moon shapes of varying sizes.
2. Stalk – Cut two 4" pieces of ⅛" light teal/white variegated paper. Cut 4" to 3" pieces to make individual stems for each flower. Scissors curl each piece.
3. Leaf – (Make 2.) For each leaf, Tear four 3" pieces from ⅛" light teal/white variegated paper. Form harp shapes, each with a small scroll at the top.
4. Scroll – (Make 1.) Cut a 2" length of ⅛" light teal/white variegated paper. Make a single scroll shape.

Decorate & Assemble:

1. Trim the corners of the purple patterned paper to make the tag shape.
2. Using a glue stick, glue the tag to the purple card. Trim, leaving a border ⅛" wide.
3. Glue the pale blue panel at the bottom of the tag.
4. Arrange the quilled elements as shown in the photo. Glue in this order: the harp shaped leaves, the stalks, and then the scroll.
5. Glue the flowers under the stems with smallest blossoms at the ends.
6. Using white glue, glue the rhinestones under the blossoms.
7. Add the rhinestone stickers.
8. Install the three eyelets to the top of the tag. Thread one of the decorative fiber pieces through each eyelet. ❏

Foxglove Card

Bell shapes made from variegated quilling strips are used to create this majestic flower.

SUPPLIES

Base:

Pink card blank, 4¼" x 5½"
(folded size)

Papers:

Quilling strips, ¼" – Pink/white
variegated

Quilling strips, ⅛" – Green

Dark brown card stock

Pink polka dot paper, 4" x 5¼"
(folded size, for a liner)

Envelope

Tools & Other Supplies:

Basic supplies and tools for quilling

Brown inkpad

Stencil brush

Rubber stamp – Script motifs

Craft knife

Metal ruler

Cutting mat

Scissors

Glue stick

INSTRUCTIONS

Make the Quilled Elements:

See the beginning of the book for detailed instructions.

1. Blossom – (Make 9.) Cut three 12" lengths of ¼" pink/white variegated quilling strips. Tear each length into 3", 3½" and 5½" pieces. Start quilling each piece from the dark end and make bell shapes.
2. Bud – (Make 3.) Tear ⅛" green quilling strips into 3" lengths. Make bell shapes.
3. Leaf – (Make 5.) Tear ⅛" green quilling strips into 3" and 4" lengths. Make leaf shapes.
4. Stem – (Make 1.) Cut a 3" length of ⅛" green quilling paper in half lengthwise to make a thin stem.

Decorate & Assemble:

1. Stamp the script design on the front of the card with brown ink.
2. Color the edges with brown ink, using a stencil brush.
3. Cut a 1⅜" x 3⅝" window in the right side of the front of the card. See "Making Card Bases."
4. Glue a dark brown paper panel behind the window. Let dry. Using a craft knife, trim away the brown paper, leaving a ⅛" border to frame the opening.
5. Tape the polka dot liner into the card. See the "Folded Liner Option" with "Making Card Bases."
6. Arrange the quilled elements, using the photo as a guide. Glue them on the polka dot paper in the window opening. Place the buds at the top of the stem, then the smaller, darker blossoms. Place the lighter, larger blossoms at the bottom. ❏

About Foxglove

A biennial, the foxglove has bell-shaped tubular flowers that bloom on tall spikes the second year after planting. The flowers vary in color and may be purple to pink, white, yellow, or coral. Its botanical name, *(Digitalis purpurea),* refers to the fact that the flowers are the size of the tip of the finger. Other names for the plant are Witches' Gloves, Dead Men's Bells, Fairy's Gloves, Fairy Thimbles.

The plant is native to Europe and a favorite of honeybees. Its leaves are the source of the heart medicine known as digitalis or digoxin. Foxglove has a history of use in herbal medicine to calm a rapid heartbeat and was first described in the medical literature in the 18th century. The plant is toxic to humans and animals, including livestock, dogs, and cats, if eaten.

Lavender Card

This lavender design, which shows the flower stalks but not the leaves, is different from the curly lavender on the Lavender Collage Card and illustrates the many ways it's possible to interpret a flower in quilled shapes.

SUPPLIES

Base:

Green card blank, 4¼" x 5½" (folded size)

Papers:

Quilling strips, ¼" – Light purple, purple

Quilling strips, ⅛" – Green

Green patterned paper, 4" x 5¼" (folded size, for a liner)

Vellum panel, 1½" x 5½", with computer-generated saying

Envelope

Tools & Other Supplies:

Basic supplies and tools for quilling

Green inkpad

Stencil brush

Craft knife

Metal ruler

Cutting mat

Scissors

Glue stick

Decorative edge scissors – Pinking, in several sizes

About Lavender

Lavender is a beautiful, fragrant perennial with gray-green foliage and flowers in various shades of purple. In the summer, the hills and valleys of the Provence region of France are colored purple by rows and rows of blooming lavender bushes. The lavender grown in Provence, which is harvested between June and September, accounts for about 70 percent of world commercial production.

Freshly cut lavender stalks are used to create the beribboned lavender wands (called *fusettes de lavande* or *fuseaux* in Provence) that are used to scent linen storage drawers and cupboards. Dried stalks are used to create wreaths and arrangements; dried buds are used for sachets and potpourris.

Lavender oil is prized as a fragrance for scenting soaps, bath oils and salts, and skincare products. Believed to be a soothing, relaxing scent, lavender is used by aromatherapists to treat irritability, depression, insomnia, and nervous tension.

INSTRUCTIONS

Make the Quilled Elements:

See the beginning of the book for detailed instructions.

1. Larger flower bud – (Make 16 in all.) Use ¼" light purple and purple quilling strips to make 8 bell shapes for each stalk.
2. Smaller flower bud – (Make 10 in all.) Use ¼" light purple and purple quilling strips to make 5 tight coils for each stalk.
3. Bud – (Make 4 in all.) Tear ⅛" green quilling strips into 3" lengths. Make 2 bell shapes for each stalk.
4. Stem – (Make 2.) Cut a 4" length of ⅛" piece of green quilling paper in half lengthwise to make two thin stems.

Decorate & Assemble:

1. Cut a 1½" x 4" window in the right side of the card front.
2. Color the edges of the window with green ink, using a stencil brush.
3. Adhere the vellum panel to the left side of the card with double sided-tape at the edges.

4. Cover the edges of the vellum and the tape with ¼" and ⅛" quilling strips, making vertical stripes on the front of the card. Cut some strips with decorative edge scissors. Use a glue stick to attach them to the card.

5. Tape the green paper liner in the card. See the "Folded Liner Option" with "Making Card Bases."

6. Glue the quilled shapes on the liner so they show through the window, using the photo as a guide. ❏

Black & Ochre Birthday Card

This unusual color combination is particularly suitable for a man's birthday.
The quilling strips for the fringed flowers are made from strips cut from
a sheet of decorative paper, rather than purchased, cut quilling strips.

SUPPLIES

Base:

Ochre card blank, 5½" x 4¼"
(folded size)

Papers:

Dictionary-patterned decorative
paper

Quilling strips, ⅛" – Black, ochre,
cream

Black paper panel, 1¼" x 4¼"

Black card stock

Vellum panel with computer-generated "Happy Birthday"

Lined envelope

Tools & Other Supplies:

Basic supplies and tools for quilling

Scissors *or* fringing tool

Ochre inkpad

Stencil brush

2 copper brads

Glue stick

Glue dots, dimensional

INSTRUCTIONS

Make the Quilled Elements:

*See the beginning of the book for
detailed instructions.*

1. Fringed flower – (Make 2.) For
each flower, cut a ⅜" x 6" strip
from dictionary-patterned decorative paper. Glue a ⅛" x 2" black
quilling strip to the end to create
the center. Color the strip with
ochre ink before quilling. See
"Making Fringed Flowers."

2. Leaf – (Make 5.) Tear ⅛" ochre
quilling strips into 3" lengths.
Make leaf shapes.

3. Scroll – (Make 8 in all.) Cut ⅛"
cream quilling strips into three 2"
lengths. Make single scrolls. Cut
⅛" black quilling strips into five
2" to 3" lengths. Make single
scrolls.

Decorate & Assemble:

1. Cut a panel 5¼" x 4" from the
dictionary-patterned paper.

2. With the glue stick, attach the
dictionary panel and black panel
to the card front.

3. Cut out one definition from the
dictionary paper. (I used "gorgeous.") Glue to black paper. Trim
the black paper to make a ⅛"
black border. Mount on the card
with dimensional glue dots.

4. Attach the vellum panel to the
card with the brads.

5. Arrange the quilled elements as
shown in the photo. Glue in place
on the card. ❏

Flowers in the Windows Card

Single blossoms placed in a row of cutout windows create this simple,
elegant card design. Varying the quilling method used on the same
variegated paper creates the color differences in the fringed flowers.

SUPPLIES

Base:

Pink card blank, 4¼" x 6"
(folded size)

Papers:

Quilling strips, ⅜" – Pink/white
variegated, pink

Quilling strips, ⅛" – Yellow

Pink patterned paper, 4⅛" x 5⅞"
(folded size, for liner)

Sticker with sentiment, ½" square

Lined envelope

Tools & Other Supplies:

Basic supplies and tools for quilling

Scissors *or* fringing tool

Craft knife

Metal ruler

Cutting mat

Double-sided tape

INSTRUCTIONS

Make the Quilled Elements:

*See the "Making Fringed Flowers" for
detailed instructions.*

Fringed flower – (Make 3 in all.) Cut
two 6" lengths of ⅜" variegated pink
quilling strip. Cut one 6" length
pink quilling strip. Glue a ⅛" x 2"
yellow quilling strip to the end of
each 6" strip to create the centers.
Quill the variegated fringed papers
from both the dark and light sides
for two different blossoms.

Decorate & Assemble:

1. Using a craft knife, cut four 1"
square windows into the right side
of the card front.
2. Attach the liner inside the card
with double-sided tape. See the
"Folded Liner Option" with
"Making Card Bases."
3. Glue the three flowers on the
lining paper in the upper three
windows.
4. Place the sticker on the lining
paper in the bottom window. ❏

Best Friends Card

The trendy color combination of brown and light blue is used for this contemporary greeting card. Word stickers related to the card's theme are arranged around the quilled elements.

SUPPLIES

Base:

Dark brown card blank,
  5½" square (folded size)

Papers:

Quilling strips, ⅜" – Blue/white variegated

Quilling strips, ⅛" – Blue/white variegated, brown/white variegated, brown

Blue polka dot patterned paper, 4" square

Sticker with sentiment, "Best Friend"

Lined envelope

Tools & Other Supplies:

Basic supplies and tools for quilling

Scissors *or* fringing tool

Rub-on letters for friendship words (e.g., "friends," "pals," "best buds")

Epoxy word stickers

Glue stick

Glue dots, dimensional

INSTRUCTIONS

Make the Quilled Elements:

See the beginning of the book for detailed instructions.

1. Fringed flower – (Make 3.) Cut ⅜" blue variegated strips into 6" lengths. Glue a ⅛" x 3" blue quilling strip to the end of each variegated strip to create the center. See "Making Fringed Flowers." Quill the variegated fringed papers from both the dark and light sides for different looks.
2. Mini paisley – (Make 6.) Tear ⅛" brown/white variegated quilling paper into 4" lengths. Make petal shapes, quilling each strip from the dark end. Make an additional twist at the end with tweezers to make the paisley shape.
3. Dot – (Make 5.) Tear ⅛" brown quilling strips into 1" lengths. Make tight coils.
4. Scroll – (Make 6.) Cut ⅛" blue/white variegated quilling strips into 1" to 3" lengths. Make single scrolls.

Inside Greetings

You can use stickers, rub-on letters, rubber stamps, a computer and printer, paint pens, or gel pens to write personalized greetings inside your cards. Here are some examples:

"Thank you for being a good friend." "Thinking of you."
"I hope we'll always be best buds." "Hope things are going well."
"You always brighten my day." "Have a wonderful day!"

Books of quotations, such as *Bartlett's Familiar Quotations,* and poetry anthologies are good sources of inspirational messages for cards. When you use a quotation or part of a poem, be sure to credit the author.

Decorate & Assemble:

1. Use a glue stick to attach the blue polka dot panel to the card.
2. Glue one variegated blue/white ⅜" quilling strip on the left side of the blue dotted panel. Glue a brown/white variegated ⅛" quilling strip on each side of the blue strip.
3. Add rub-on friendship words to the variegated blue strip.
4. Attach the "best friends" sticker to dark brown paper. Trim, leaving a ⅛" border. Attach to card with dimensional glue dots.
5. Arrange the quilled elements as shown and glue in place.
6. Attach the epoxy stickers to the card. ❑

Joy Card

In addition to the huge number of decorative papers available, you can make your own papers for your card creations. Don't be afraid to experiment! This card is an example of an original decorative paper design created with a stencil, stamps, and ink.

You can also cut your own stencil from freezer paper, using a circle template and shape cutter. Place the freezer paper stencil shiny side up when stenciling.

SUPPLIES

Base:

Bright blue card blank, 5½" x 4¼" (folded size)

Papers:

Quilling strips, ⅜" – Teal/white variegated, green/white variegated

Quilling strips, ⅛" – Green

Bright green panel, 5¼" x 4"

Text weight paper – Bright blue, bright green (for punching)

Alphabet stickers – J, O, Y

Lined envelope

Tools & Other Supplies:

Basic supplies and tools for quilling

Scissors *or* fringing tool

Decorative flower punches, 1" and ½" diameters

Inkpads – White, dark green

Stencil brush

Rubber stamp – Swirl flourish

Stencil – Circle and flower

Rhinestone stickers

Dimensional glue dots

INSTRUCTIONS

Make the Quilled Elements:

See the beginning of the book for detailed instructions.

1. Fringed flower – (Make 4 in all.) Cut ⅜" teal/ white variegated and green/white variegated quilling paper into 6" lengths. Cut two 3" lengths of ⅛" green quilling paper and glue to two of the 6" lengths. See "Making Fringed Flowers." Make two fringed flowers without centers and two fringed flowers with green centers.
2. Small fringed flower – (Make 3.) Cut green/white variegated quilling paper into 3" lengths. Make small fringed flowers.
3. Scroll – (Make 5.) Cut ⅛" teal/white variegated quilling strips into 1" to 3" lengths. Make single scroll shapes. Scissors curl the tail of each in the opposite direction of the scroll to create the soft S-curve.

Decorate & Assemble:

1. Punch four large flowers and three small from blue and green papers.
2. Glue the punched shapes to the bottoms of the fringed flowers.
3. Create a design on the green paper panel with white ink, using a stencil brush and the circle and flower stencil. Use the photo as a guide for stencil placement.
4. Stamp the flourish motif on the green panel with green ink. Use the photo as a guide for placement.
5. Arrange the quilled elements, using the photo as a guide. Glue in place on the card.
6. Adhere the J-O-Y stickers to bright blue paper. Trim around the letters, leaving small borders. Attach them to the card with the dimensional glue dots.
7. Add rhinestone stickers to flower centers and the stamped flourishes. ❑

Mom Card

Chipboard letters – decorated with acrylic colors and dimensional varnish – add dimension to a card. This design – letters decorated with flowers and quilling – could also be done with other short words (Joy, Baby, Cute, Dad, Love, Life, etc.).

SUPPLIES

Base:

Bright blue card blank, 5½" x 4¼" (folded size)

Papers:

Quilling strips, ⅜" – Red/pink variegated

Quilling strips, ⅛" – Pink, bright green, blue, purple

Light purple card stock, 5¼" x 4"

Lined envelope

Tools & Other Supplies:

Basic supplies and tools for quilling

Scissors *or* fringing tool

Clear dimensional varnish

Metallic gold inkpad

Stencil brush

Rhinestones – Dark blue, clear

Metallic watercolor paints and applicator

Dimensional glue dots

Chipboard letters – M,O,M

Acrylic craft paints – Bright green, teal

Paint brushes

INSTRUCTIONS

Make the Quilled Elements:

See the beginning of the book for detailed instructions.

1. Fringed flower – (Make 1.) Cut a 6" length of ⅜" red/pink variegated quilling paper. Glue a ⅛" x 3" pink quilling strip to the end of the strip to create the center. See "Making Fringed Flowers."

2. Green leaf – (Make 7.) Tear ⅛" bright green quilling paper into 4" lengths. Make eye shapes.

3. Blue leaf – (Make 2.) Tear ⅛" blue quilling strips into 6" lengths. Make eccentric teardrop shapes.

4. Scroll – (Make 6.) Cut ⅛" purple quilling strips into 1" to 2" lengths. Make single scrolls.

Decorate & Assemble:

1. Paint the chipboard letters with acrylic paints. Brush each letter with both colors to create a mottled look. Let dry.

2. Apply clear dimensional varnish to the letters for a high gloss finish. Let dry.

3. Color the edges of the light purple card panel with gold ink, using the stencil brush.

4. Glue a dark blue rhinestone in the center of the fringed flower.

5. Glue three clear rhinestones on one letter "M."

6. Attach the letters to the card with dimensional glue dots.

7. Using the photo as a guide, arrange the quilled elements, tucking some under the raised letters. Glue in place.

8. Paint the tops of the quilled shapes with gold watercolors. ❏

Rose in a Window Card

A single rose in a cutout window is accented with rhinestone dewdrops.
It would be a lovely card for Mother's Day or a birthday.

SUPPLIES

Base:

Light pink card blank, 4¼" x 6"
(folded size)

Papers:

Quilling strips, ⅛" – Green/white
variegated

White card stock

Pink polka dot patterned paper,
4⅛" x 5⅞" (folded size, for liner)

Lined envelope

Tools & Other Supplies:

Basic supplies and tools for quilling

Basic supplies and tools for swirl
flowers

Craft knife

Metal ruler

Cutting mat

Inkpads – Green, pink

Stencil brushes

Rubber stamp with fern motif

Double-sided tape

3 clear rhinestones

Tiny gold beads

Embossing pad

Embossing tool

Decorative edge scissors – Large
scallop (cloud)

Decorative punch – Leaf, ½" long

INSTRUCTIONS

Make the Rose:

See "Making Swirl Flowers" for detailed instructions.

1. Stamp the spiral design on the back of the white card stock.
2. Color the front with pink ink, using a stencil brush.
3. Cut the swirl with decorative scallop scissors and form into a rose.
4. Glue tiny gold beads in the center.

Make the Scrolls & Leaves:

See the beginning of the book for detailed instructions.

1. Scroll – (Make 3.) Cut ⅛" white/green variegated quilling strips into 1" to 1½" lengths. Make single scrolls.
2. Leaf – Color white paper with green ink. See "Coloring Paper." Punch six leaf motifs from the colored paper. Shape the six leaves on an embossing pad.

Decorate & Assemble:

1. Cut a 2" square window in the card front, using a craft knife.
2. Attach the liner paper inside the card with double-sided tape. See the "Folded Liner Option" with "Making Card Bases."
3. With the fern rubber stamp and green inkpad, stamp three ferns in the center of the window on the liner paper.
4. Arrange the rose, quilled scrolls, and shaped leaves in the card window on the liner paper. Glue in place.
5. Glue the rhinestones in place, using the photo as a guide. ❏

Roses in an Oval Card

Two roses surrounded by quilled scrolls, shaped paper leaves, and
rhinestones are arranged in and around an oval cutout.

SUPPLIES

Base:

Light pink card blank, 5½" x 4¼"
(folded size)

Papers:

Quilling strips, ⅛" – Green/white
variegated

White card stock

Green polka dot paper, 5¼" x 4"

Lined envelope

Tools & Other Supplies:

Basic supplies and tools for quilling

Basic supplies and tools for swirl
flowers

Shape cutter and oval template

Glue stick

Inkpads – Green, pink

Stencil brushes

Rubber stamp with fern motif

Rhinestone swirl stickers

Tiny gold beads

Decorative edge scissors – Large
scallop (cloud)

Decorative punch – ½" long leaf

Embossing tool

Embossing pad

INSTRUCTIONS

Make the Rose:

See "Making Swirl Flowers" for detailed instructions.

1. Stamp two spiral designs on the back of the white card stock.
2. Color the fronts with pink ink, using a stencil brush.
3. Cut out the swirls with decorative scallop scissors and form into one large
   rose and one medium-size rose.
4. Glue tiny gold beads in the center.

Make the Scrolls & Leaves:

See the beginning of the book for detailed instructions.

1. Scroll – (Make 7.) Cut ⅛" white/green variegated quilling strips into 1" to
   1½" lengths. Make single scrolls.
2. Leaf – Color white paper with green ink. See "Coloring Paper." Punch
   seven leaf motifs from the colored paper. Shape the seven leaves on an
   embossing pad.

About Roses

The rose is called the "queen of flowers." Roses symbolize happy love. In
Victorian times, friends and lovers used the symbolic meanings of different flowers to send a special message. Red roses were expressions of love,
pink roses expressed friendship, and white roses conveyed the message "I
am worthy of you."

Roses grow in a variety of forms and colors. The upright bush roses are
known as hybrid teas and grandifloras. Floribundas, which bloom in
clusters, grow on smaller bushes. Climbing roses must be trained to grow
or fastened to a support of some kind (a tree, a fence, or a trellis, for
example).

Beautiful to behold, roses have a long tradition in perfumery and aro-
matherapy. It takes over 500 pounds of rose petals to make one pound of
rose concentrate, and 5,000 pounds of petals to make a pound of rose
essential oil. Aromatherapists consider rose oil to be antidepressant,
aphrodisiac, balancing, and spiritual. It is a lovely addition to skin care
products – especially those for mature skin – and massage oils.

Decorate & Assemble:

1. Cut a 2½" x 3½" oval window in the green polka dot paper panel.
2. Glue the dotted panel with the cutout oval window to the front of the card with a glue stick. Glue the cutout oval piece inside the card.
3. Using the fern rubber stamp with green ink, stamp four ferns in the center of the oval window.
4. Arrange the roses, quilled scrolls, and shaped leaves in and around the oval window. Glue in place.
5. Glue the rhinestone accents to the card, using the photo as a guide. ❏

Always Laugh Together Card

The words and roses on this card are placed in a seemingly random fashion that lends movement to the design, giving the appearance that the roses are tumbling down the card.

SUPPLIES

Base:

Light blue card blank, 4¼" x 5½" (folded size)

Papers:

Quilling strips, ⅛" – Blue/white variegated

White card stock

Bright blue paper

Lined envelope

Tools & Other Supplies:

Basic supplies and tools for quilling

Basic supplies and tools for swirl flowers

Decorative edge scissors – Large scallop (cloud)

Leaf rubber stamp, 1" long

Epoxy word stickers

Inkpads – Green, purple, blue

Stencil brushes

Embossing pad

Embossing tool

1 yd. variegated blue/white narrow ribbon

Glue stick

Clear rhinestones

INSTRUCTIONS

Make the Roses:

See "Making Swirl Flowers" for detailed instructions.

1. Stamp three spirals on the back of the white card stock.
2. Color the fronts with purple and blue inks.
3. Cut out with decorative scissors and form into three roses.
4. Glue a rhinestone into each center.

Make the Scrolls & Leaves:

See the beginning of the book for detailed instructions.

1. Scroll – (Make 3.) Cut ⅛" blue/white variegated quilling strips into 2" lengths. Make single scrolls.
2. Leaves – Stamp three leaf motifs on white card stock. Color with green ink. Cut out and shape on the embossing pad.

Decorate & Assemble:

1. Cut three 1½" squares from bright blue paper. Using the photo as a guide, glue them down the right side of the card.
2. Place the epoxy word stickers on bright blue paper. Trim around the stickers, leaving a ⅛" border. Glue on the left side of the card front.
3. Arrange the roses, scrolls, and leaves on the blue squares. Glue in place.
4. Wrap the ribbon around the fold of the card. Trim the end and glue to secure. Make three small bows from the remaining ribbon and glue as shown in the photo.
5. Glue the rhinestone accents on the card. ❏

Kindred Spirit Card

The quilled and paper sculpted elements were inspired by the design of the decorative paper. What other creative ideas might sheets of paper inspire?

SUPPLIES

Base:

Light blue card blank, 5½" x 4¼" (folded size)

Paper:

Quilling strips, ⅛" – Dark brown, yellow

Red card stock

Patterned card stock

Stickers (clear backing) with sentiments

Lined envelope

Tools & Other Supplies:

Basic supplies and tools for quilling

Basic supplies and tools for swirl flowers

Decorative edge scissors – Large scallop (cloud)

Decorative punch – ½" flower

Watercolor paint – Iridescent silver

Watercolor paint applicator

Glue stick

Small flower beads with pearl finish

Mini yellow pom-pom

INSTRUCTIONS

Make the Quilled Elements:

See the beginning of the book for detailed instructions.

1. Scroll – (Make 3.) Cut ⅛" brown quilling strips into 2" lengths. Make single scrolls.
2. Leaf – (Make 3.) Tear ⅛" yellow quilling strips into 4" lengths. Make leaf shapes.

Make the Flowers:

1. Stamp the spiral design on red card stock.
2. Cut out with decorative scissors and form into a rose.
3. Glue the pom-pom in the center.
4. Punch three flowers from red card stock and three from patterned card stock. Shape on the embossing pad. Glue two – one of each type of paper – together to make three two-color blossoms.

Decorate & Assemble:

1. From the patterned card stock, cut a panel 5¼" x 4" and a strip 1" x 4¼".
2. With the glue stick, attach the patterned panel to the front of the card.
3. Glue the patterned strip on the red paper. Trim, leaving a narrow border on each side of the strip. Glue to the front of the card.
4. Using the photo as a guide, glue the quilled leaves and scrolls and the swirl flowers and punched flowers to the card.
5. Paint the tops of the quilled elements and paper flowers with silver watercolors.
6. Add the sayings stickers to the card. ❑

Laugh!

Shaped punched flowers are a simple, quick embellishment for cards – and envelopes. I used rub-on lettering to write "Laugh" on the front of the card, but you could use any lettering method to customize your card design.

SUPPLIES

Base:

Light green card, 4¼" x 6"
    (folded size)

Papers:

Green polka dot decorative paper

Green paper

Lined envelope

Tools & Other Supplies:

Craft knife

Metal ruler

Cutting mat

Decorative punch – Daisy petals,
    1" diameter

Embossing pad

Embossing tool

5 mini pom-poms – Bright green

Rub-on lettering

Double-sided tape

INSTRUCTIONS

Make the Flowers:

See "Making Shaped Paper."

1. Punch five daisies from green paper.
2. Punch five daisies from green polka dot paper.
3. Shape the daisies on the embossing pad.
4. Glue one of each type of paper together to make five blossoms.
5. Glue a mini pom-pom in the center of each flower.

Decorate & Assemble:

1. With a craft knife, cut four 1" square windows down the right side of the card.
2. Cut a panel from polka dot paper measuring 8" x 5¾". Fold to make a liner 4" x 5¾". Tape the liner inside the card. See the "Folded Liner Option" with "Making Card Bases."

3. Add rub-on lettering to the bottom of the card.
4. Glue one blossom on the lining paper in each cutout window so the flowers show through the windows.
5. Glue the remaining flower on the envelope flap. ❏

Bag of Daisies Birthday Card

Punched flowers with quilled centers, leaves, and stems and a twine-tied paper bag decorate a birthday card. There's no need to hunt for mini brown bags – you can make your own with the pattern provided.

SUPPLIES

Base:

Kraft card blank, 5" x 7" (folded size)

Papers:

Quilling strips, ⅛" – Yellow, green

Piece of brown paper bag *or* brown kraft paper, 4" x 5"

White card stock (for punching)

Envelope to match card

Tools & Other Supplies:

Basic supplies and tools for quilling

Decorative edge scissors – Mini pinking

Decorative punch – Daisy, 1" diameter

Brown inkpad

Stencil brush

Embossing pad

Embossing tool

Rub-on lettering – Birthday theme

Glue stick

Scissors

Waxed linen cord

PATTERN

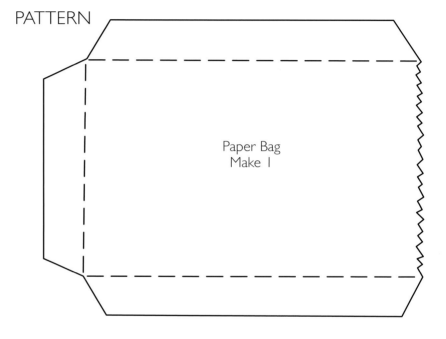

Paper Bag
Make 1

INSTRUCTIONS

Make the Quilled Elements:

See the beginning of the book for detailed instructions.

1. Stem – (Make 7.) Cut ⅛" green quilling paper into 2" to 3" lengths. Curl slightly with scissors.
2. Leaf – (Make 5.) Tear ⅛" green quilling paper into 4" lengths. Make teardrop shapes.
3. Scroll – (Make 4.) Cut ⅛" green quilling paper into 1" lengths. Make single scrolls.
4. Flower center – (Make 7.) Tear ⅛" yellow quilling paper into 4" lengths. Make tight coils.
5. Peg (for dimension) – (Make 7.) Tear ⅛" yellow quilling paper into 3" lengths. Make tight coils.

Make the Flowers:

See "Making Shaped Paper."

1. Punch seven daisies from white card stock.
2. Shape the flowers on the embossing pad.
3. Glue a yellow coil in the center of each blossom.

Decorate & Assemble:

1. Crumple the brown paper piece and smooth flat.
2. Using the pattern provided, cut out the bag shape. Trim the top edge with mini pinking decorative scissors.
3. Fold under the flaps. Color the edges of the bag piece with brown ink, using a stencil brush.
4. Add rub-on lettering to the front of the bag and the front of the card.
5. Tie a piece of waxed linen around the bag and finish with a bow.
6. Using a glue stick, attach the bag to the front of the card.
7. Glue a green peg to the back of each daisy and glue the daisies to the card.
8. Glue the stems, leaves, and scrolls in place, using the photo as a guide.
9. Accent the envelope flap with one of the negative punched pieces. ❑

happy birthday

cel•ebr te (se . t.
1. 2. to memorate
(holiday or birthday)
w 3. t onor publicly—
to ave ood ti .

party (pär't 1. a group of
people work to promote a
political platfor 2. to attend or
hold a celebratio for a person

wish (wish)
a longing for
a desire conc
request; to long for

celebrate

Happy Birthday Daisies

You could use this cheery card design to spell out all kinds of greetings, such as
"Happy Anniversary," "Get Well," or (if you make a field of blossoms) an entire quotation.
The punched daisies are glued flat with no shaping. Quilling paper is used for the stems.

SUPPLIES

Base:

Bright green card blank, 5½" x 4¼" (folded size)

Papers:

Quilling paper strips, ⅛" – Light green

Bright blue paper (for punching)

Light purple paper (for punching)

Lined envelope

Tools & Other Supplies:

Decorative punches – Flower, ½" diameter

Alphabet beads to spell "Happy Birthday"

White glue

Glue stick

INSTRUCTIONS

1. Punch five daisies from light purple paper. Punch eight daises from bright blue paper.
2. Cut five 4" pieces and eight 3" pieces of green quilling paper.
3. With the glue stick, glue the light purple daisies in an uneven line on the card front. Immediately glue a 4" piece of green quilling paper under each daisy, letting the excess hang over the edge of the card.
4. Glue the blue daisies under the light purple daisies in an uneven line. Immediately glue a 3" piece of green quilling paper under each daisy, letting the excess hang over the edge of the card. **Note:** If a blue daisy is placed so it shares a stem with a light purple daisy, you don't need to add another stem.
5. Using scissors, trim off the parts of the quilling strips overhanging the card.
6. With white glue, attach an alphabet bead at the center of each flower.
7. *Optional:* Decorate the envelope flap with punched daisies and stems. ❑

About Daisies

Members of the chrysanthemum family, daisies are a composite flower with a round, well-defined center encircled by ray flowers that are the petals. Though the shasta daisy *(Chrysanthemum x superbum),* with its bright white petals and yellow-gold center, is the most familiar, there are dozens of varieties of daisies with petals and centers of many colors and sizes.

Painted daisies *(C. coccineum),* with petals of pink, rose, or red, are the source of the pyrethrin insecticide used to kill aphids, flies, and mosquitos. The Clara Curtis daisy *Chrysanthemum x rubellum)* has pink petals and a yellow center. Another white-petaled daisy is the oxeye *(C. leucanthemum),* a familiar roadside plant that grows best in average soil and blooms for two to three months, beginning in early spring.

Shasta daisies' white petals brighten the flower garden, and they make great cut flowers when massed in vases or used as part of an arrangement.

Artful Thanks

A bright and bold card for your colorful acquaintances!

SUPPLIES

Base:

Bright green card blank, 5½" x 4¼" (folded size)

Papers:

Bright blue paper

Purple paper (for punching)

Blue paper (for punching)

Paper cutout letters *or* rub-on letters to spell "thanks!"

Lined envelope

Tools & Other Supplies:

Paper trimmer

Decorative punches – Fat-petaled flower, 1" and ½" diameters

Embossing pad

Embossing tool

5 purple mini pom-poms

Glue stick

INSTRUCTIONS

Make the Sculptured Flowers:

See "Making Shaped Paper" for detailed instructions.

1. Punch five 1" flowers from purple paper.
2. Punch five ½" flowers from blue paper.
3. Shape the flower petals on the embossing pad.
4. Glue one large and small flower together to make five blossoms.
5. Glue a mini pom-pom in the center of each blossom.

Decorate & Assemble:

1. Use a paper trimmer to cut out five uneven squares from bright blue paper. Glue them along the bottom of the card.
2. Add the letters about the blue paper pieces.
3. Glue the blossoms in a row – one in the middle of each blue paper piece.
4. Decorate the envelope flap with the remaining daisy. ❏

Blue Daisies

Using the paper coloring technique allows you to change the colors of this design for a vast assortment of different cards. (See "Coloring Paper" for detailed instructions.) Don't throw away the negative paper shapes that remain after you've punched the daisies – use them to accent the envelope or the inside of the card.

SUPPLIES

Base:

Blue card blank, 4¼" x 5½" (folded size)

Papers:

Bright green paper, 2½" square

White card stock (for punching)

Lined envelope

Paper trimmer

Decorative punches – Daisy, 1" and ½" diameters

Blue inkpad

Stencil brush

Embossing pad

Embossing tool

10 clear rhinestones

Purple gel pen

Glue stick

Dimensional glue dots

INSTRUCTIONS

Make the Flowers:

See "Making Shaped Paper" for detailed instructions.

1. Color the white paper from dark to light with blue ink, using a stencil brush.
2. Punch nine 1" daisies from and nine ½" daisies from the colored paper.
3. Shape the flower petals on the embossing pad.
4. Glue together one of each size to make nine blossoms.
5. Glue a clear rhinestone in the center of each blossom.

Decorate & Assemble:

1. Color the edges of the front of the card with blue ink, using a stencil brush.
2. Glue the green square to the card.
3. Add a message with the purple gel pen around the green panel. I used the short poem "Sun shines, birds sing, garden angels, flowers bring."
4. Arrange the flowers by color, placing the darkest-color daisy in the top left corner and the lightest-color daisy in the lower right corner. Attach the flowers to the green panel with dimensional glue dots.
5. Accent the envelope flap with a square of card stock under a negative punched piece. Glue the remaining rhinestone in the center. ❏

Hydrangea Cards

Hydrangea blossoms are my favorite sculpted paper flower. I use different color combinations for the blossoms, such as purple and green, shades of green, and green and pink. You can choose your own custom color combinations.

SUPPLIES

Base:

Card blank, 4¼" x 5½" (folded size)

Papers:

Paper for panels (Choose a color that contrasts with the card.)

Cream card stock

Green card stock

Quilling paper strips, ⅛" – Green

Tools & Other Supplies:

Decorative punches – Blossom, ½" diameter; Leaf, ¾" long x ½" wide

Inkpads – Green, flower colors (pink, purple, blue)

Stencil brushes

Brads – 6 per card in a matching color

Peel-off stickers *or* gel pen *or* calligraphy marker (for lettering)

Seed beads

Embossing pad

Embossing tool

INSTRUCTIONS

Make the Flowers:

See "Coloring Paper" and "Making Shaped Paper" for detailed instructions.

1. Color the cream paper with flower-color inks, using stencil brushes to blend one color into the next.

2. Punch 18 (for a smaller cluster) to 32 (for a larger flower cluster or for two clusters) blossom shapes from the colored paper.

3. Shape the flowers on the embossing pad.

4. Using white glue, adhere a seed bead in the center of each blossom.

Make the Leaves:

1. Color the green card stock with a lighter green ink or the same flower color inks as the blossoms. See "Coloring Paper."

2. Punch four to five leaves from the colored green card stock.

3. Shape the leaves on the embossing pad.

Decorate & Assemble:

1. From the contrasting color paper, cut two panels, one 3½" x 4¼" and one 3½" x ¾".

Continued on page 86

Hydrangea macrophylla

Happy Birthday

Best Wishes

Continued from page 84

2. Color the edges of the panels with ink, using a stencil brush. Choose one of the blossom colors or brown, for an antique effect.

3. Add a greeting to the small panel.

4. With a glue stick, glue the panels to the card front.

5. Install brads at each corner of the larger panel and on the ends of the smaller panel.

6. Arrange the shaped blossoms in a dome shape towards the top of the larger panel with the lighter blossoms on the left and the darker blossoms on the right with the colors blending evenly.

7. Cut six to eight 3" lengths of ⅛" green quilling paper for stems.

8. Dip one end of each strip in white glue and position in the blossoms. Let dry completely. Glue the strips together to form the main stem, using the photo as a guide.

9. Place the stems and blossoms on the card. Trim the ends of the stems as needed. Glue in place.

10. Glue the shaped leaves below the blossoms, using the photo as a guide for placement. ❏

Photo Card

Rows of blossoms make a perfect frame for a favorite photo. This is a great grandma card!

SUPPLIES

Base:

Blue card blank, 4¼" x 5½" (folded size)

Papers:

Blue paper (slightly darker than the card)

White card stock (for punching)

Blue card stock (for punching)

Photo, 2" square

Lined envelope

Tools & Other Supplies:

Craft knife

Metal ruler

Cutting mat

Decorative punch – Daisy, ½" diameter

Blue inkpad

Stencil brush

Embossing pad

Embossing tool

Clear rhinestones

Glue stick

INSTRUCTIONS

Make the Flowers:

See "Making Shaped Paper" for detailed instructions.

1. Punch 16 daisies from blue card stock.
2. Color the white card stock with blue ink, using a stencil brush.
3. Punch 16 daisies from the colored card stock.
4. Shape the blue colored-paper daisies on the embossing pad.
5. Glue a shaped daisy on a flat blue daisy.
6. Glue a clear rhinestone in the center of each blossom.

Decorate & Assemble:

1. With a craft knife, cut a 2½" square window on the card front. Set aside the cutout piece.
2. Cut a panel 4" x 5¼" from the darker blue paper. Tape the blue paper panel on the inside front of the card. Be sure no tape shows through the window.
3. Cut a 1½" square window in the middle of the darker blue window.
4. Glue the photograph in the window.
5. Cover the back of the photo with the reserved 2½" square cut from the card front.
6. Glue the blossoms, evenly spaced, along the edge of the larger window.
7. Decorate the envelope flap with three daisies punched from the darker blue paper. *Optional:* Glue a rhinestone in the center of each daisy. ❏

Hoppy Birthday Frog Card

This hoppy little guy is fun to make and can be arranged on the card in many different ways. Here, he's jumping for his dinner.

SUPPLIES

Base:

Bright blue card blank, 5½" x 6" (folded size)

Papers:

Quilling strips, ¼" – Green/white variegated, red, white, black

Light blue card stock, 5" x 5¾"

Tools & Other Supplies:

Basic supplies and tools for quilling

Basic supplies and tools for husking

Shape cutter and square template

Cutting mat

Inkpads – Green, blue

Stencil brushes

Rubber stamps – Alphabet

14" decorative fibers – Green and blue

2 googly eyes

INSTRUCTIONS

Make the Husked Elements:

See "Husking" for detailed instructions.

Using the patterns provided, make the frog's body, leg sections, and feet from ¼" green/white variegated quilling strips.

Make the Quilled Elements:

See the beginning of the book for detailed instructions.

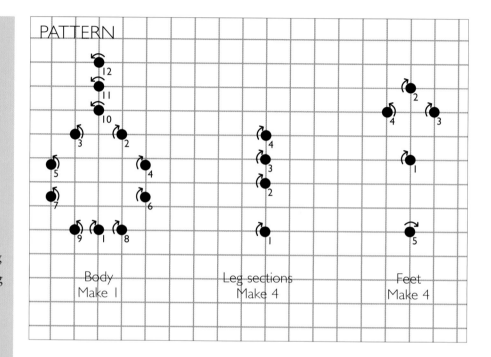

PATTERN

Body
Make 1

Leg sections
Make 4

Feet
Make 4

1. Eye – (Make 2.) Tear ¼" green/white variegated quilling strips into 3" lengths. Make loose coils. Glue a googly eye on top of each coil.
2. Tongue – (Make 1.) Cut a 3" length of ¼" red quilling strip. Make a single scroll.
3. Fly – (Make 1.) Tear a 6" piece of black quilling paper. Make one tight coil. Tear two 3" pieces of white quilling paper. Make two teardrop shapes.

Decorate & Assemble:

1. Cut a 4½" square window in the front of the bright blue card, using the photo as a guide for placement.

2. Color the edges of the card with green and blue inks, using stencil brushes.
3. Stamp "Hoppy Birthday" at the bottom of the card, using the alphabet stamps with blue and green ink.
4. Attach the light blue panel behind the window.
5. Arrange the husked frog pieces as shown in the photo. Use all four leg sections for the back legs. Cut additional pieces of quilling strips for the front legs.
6. Glue the husked and quilled elements on the light blue card stock as shown.
7. Tie the decorative fibers around the fold of the card. ❏

Ladybug Good Luck Card

Ladybugs are lucky bugs. This fun card will brighten up anyone's day.

SUPPLIES

Base:
Red card blank, 5½" square
(folded size)

Papers:
Quilling strips, ¼" – Black, red
White card stock
Red card stock
Light blue card stock

Tools & Other Supplies:
Basic supplies and tools for quilling
Basic supplies and tools for husking
Shape cutter and circle template
Cutting mat
Black inkpad
Rubber stamps – Alphabet
⅓ yd. black polka dot ribbon
⅓ yd. red rick rack
2 googly eyes
Glue stick

INSTRUCTIONS

Make the Husked Elements:
See "Husking" for detailed instructions.
1. Make the ladybug's body, using ¼" red quilling strips and following the pattern provided.
2. Make the ladybug's head, using ¼" black quilling strips and following the pattern provided. Glue the googly eyes on top of the head.
3. Make the ladybug's legs, using ¼" black quilling strips and following the pattern provided.

Make the Quilled Elements:
See the beginning of the book for detailed instructions.
1. Black dot – (Make 5 in all.) Tear ¼" black quilling strips into 2½" lengths. Make three tight coils and two loose coils.
2. Feeler – (Make 2.) Cut ¼" black quilling strips into 1" lengths. Make single scrolls.

PATTERN

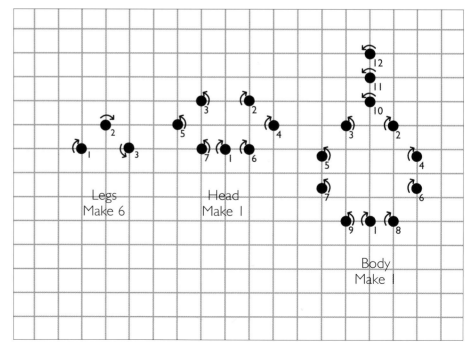

Decorate & Assemble:

1. Cut a 4" circle from white card stock. Glue it on the front of the card.

2. Cut a 3" circle from red card stock. Glue it on the white circle, positioning it off-center as shown.

3. Cut a 2½" circle from light blue card stock. Glue it on the red circle.

4. Rubber stamp "Good Luck" along the upper edge of the white circle.

5. Arrange the husked and quilled elements and glue to the light blue circle.

6. Glue the dotted ribbon and the red rick rack along the side of the card near the fold. ❑

Home Decor
&
Gift Projects

You can also decorate surfaces such as small canvas boards, wooden frames, journal covers, scrapbook pages, tins, or paper tags to showcase your quilling and paper sculpting skills. This section contains a variety of ideas for paper projects that would make lovely additions to your rooms or someone else's.

...nfidently in ... ...tion
...dreams. Live ... ...you
have imagined.

Lavandula angustifolia

Zinnia Containers

These little glass-topped tins would make perfect hostess gifts. Fill them with beaded wine-glass charms or a pair of beaded earrings. I wrapped ribbons around bottoms of the tins for an easy, finished look.

SUPPLIES

Base:

2 round glass-topped watchmaker's tins, one 2", one 1¾"

Papers:

White card stock

Blue and green decorative paper

Tools & Other Supplies:

Basic supplies and tools for swirl flowers

Decorative edge scissors – Stamp edge

Scissors

Embossing pad

Embossing tool

Inkpads – Green, blue

Stencil brushes

Decorative punch – Leaf, ½"

Stickers – Silver leaf scrolls

⅛ yd. green polka dot ribbon

⅛ yd. green and blue tartan ribbon

INSTRUCTIONS

Make the Flowers:

See "Making Fringed Flowers" for detailed instructions.

1. Stamp the spiral design on the back of the white card stock.
2. Turn over and color with green and blue inks. See "Coloring Paper."
3. Cut out the flowers with stamp edge decorative scissors. Fringe between the motifs.
4. Form into two zinnia blossoms.

Make the Leaves:

See "Making Shaped Paper."

1. Punch six leaf shapes from blue and green decorative paper.
2. Shape on the embossing pad. Glue two leaf shapes together. Make three leaves per tin.

Decorate & Assemble:

1. Put the silver stickers on the tops.
2. Cut circles from the blue and green decorative paper to line the bottoms of tins. TIP: Use the tin as a template – draw a pencil line around the tin on the back of the paper and cut out with scissors.
3. Glue the zinnias on the centers of the lids. Add the shaped leaves. ❏

Flowers on an Easel

This little masterpiece makes a perfect accent for a desk or shelf. If you can't find
a peel-off pot sticker, use a vase sticker or a stamped image of a vase or a pot.

SUPPLIES

Base:

Foam core board, 3" square

Cream handmade paper with
embossed gold dots, 5" square

Cream card stock, 2⅞" square
(for backing)

Mini easel

Papers:

Quilling strips, ⅜" – Pink/white
variegated, pink

Quilling strips, ⅛" –
Bright green, blue,
purple

Bright green card stock
(for punching)

Green pearl card stock
(for punching)

Cream paper

Tools & Other Supplies:

Basic supplies and tools
for quilling

Scissors *or* fringing tool

Embossing pad

Embossing tool

Decorative punch –
Fern; leaf, ½"

14" pink and brown
ribbon, ½" wide

Stickers – Pots, pail,
mini bees

Brown inkpad

Stencil brush

Dimensional glue dots

Glue stick

INSTRUCTIONS

Make the Paper Elements:

See the beginning of the book for detailed instructions.

1. Fringed flower – (Make 3, 2 with centers.) Cut 6" lengths of ⅜" pink/white
   variegated strips. Glue a 3" length of ⅛" pink quilling strip on two fringed
   strips to create the centers. See "Making Fringed Flowers."
2. Fringed bud – (Make 2.) Tear ⅜" pink/white variegated quilling strips into 3"
   lengths. Make two fringed buds.
3. Calyx – (Make 1 for each bud.) Tear ⅛" bright green quilling strips into 4"
   lengths. Make into bells. Glue a bell to the bottom of each fringed bud.
4. Leaf – (Make 6.) Punch leaves from bright green paper. Shape on an
   embossing pad.
5. Fern – (Make 5.) Punch fern motifs from green pearl paper.

Decorate & Assemble:

1. Cover the foam core piece with
   handmade paper, using a glue
   stick and folding the excess
   paper to the back.
2. Cover the back with the cream
   card stock piece.
3. Place the pots and pail stickers
   on cream paper. Shade the edges
   with brown ink. Cut out.
4. Cut a scrap piece of paper to use
   as a mask. Use a stencil brush to
   color a line near the bottom of
   the paper-covered square to
   create a table top.
5. Attach the pots and pail cutouts
   to the canvas with dimensional
   glue dots.
6. Glue the ferns, flowers, leaves,
   and buds in place, using the
   photo as a guide for placement.
7. Apply the bee peel-off stickers.
8. Wrap the edges of the board
   with ribbon and glue in place
   with white glue. Let dry. Place
   the finished piece on the easel. ❏

Wedding Tin

All the different types of paper elements – quilling, swirl roses, punched blossoms, and husking – can be arranged together with good results, as seen in this charming covered tin. It's a perfect container for a wedding music CD or DVD memory gift.

SUPPLIES

Base:

Compact disc tin, 5" diameter

Papers:

Quilling strips, ⅛" – White

Off-white decorative paper

Pearl white card stock

White patterned vellum

Tools & Other Supplies:

Basic supplies and tools for quilling

Basic supplies and tools for swirl flowers

Basic supplies and tools for husking

Decorative edge scissors – Large scallop (cloud), decorative scallop (seagull)

Embossing pad

Embossing tool

Silver pearl inkpad

Stencil brush

Decorative punches – Leaf, ½"; blossom, ½"

Stickers – Silver scroll

Clear rhinestones

Glue stick

Double-sided tape

½ yd. silver iridescent wire-edge ribbon, ⅛" wide

Compass and pencil

INSTRUCTIONS

Make the Swirl Rose:

1. Stamp the spiral on the back of the off-white paper.
2. Turn over and color with silver pearl ink. See "Coloring Paper."
3. Cut out with large scallop decorative scissors.
4. Form into a rose.
5. Glue a rhinestone at the center.

Punch the Blossoms & Leaves:

1. Color off-white paper with silver ink, using a stencil brush.
2. Punch three blossoms and four leaves from the silver-colored paper.
3. Shape all the punched pieces on an embossing pad.
4. Glue a rhinestone in the center of each blossom.

Make the Husked Elements:

See the beginning of the book for detailed instructions.

Wheatears – (Make 3 (1 with a scroll).) With ⅛" white quilling paper, husk three wheatears with loops spaced ¼" apart. See "Husking."

Make the Fringed Flower:

See "Making Fringed Flowers."

1. Cut a 6" strip of off-white decorative paper ⅜" wide.
2. Color with silver pearl ink.
3. Fringe the strip.
4. Glue a 2" length of ⅛" white quilling paper to the end to create the center. Make the flower.
5. Glue a rhinestone in the center.

Decorate & Assemble:

1. Draw a circle 4¾" in diameter on white pearl paper. Cut out with decorative scallop scissors. Glue to the top of the tin.
2. Draw a circle 4¼" in diameter on off-white paper. Cut out with large scallop scissors. Glue to the top of the tin.
3. Draw a circle 4" in diameter on vellum paper. Cut out. Adhere to the top of the tin by placing a piece of double-sided tape in the center.
4. Place the silver scroll peel-off stickers on the top of the paper circles.
5. Arrange the paper elements on the top of the tin and glue in place. Use the photo as a guide for placement.
6. Glue clear rhinestones to the silver scroll stickers.
7. Make a multi-loop bow with the ribbon. Fold in half. Glue under the swirl rose. ❑

Framed Botanicals

These framed quilled and paper sculpted flower arrangements have an old world charm. The three flowers are lavender, hydrangea, and foxglove. Note how different – in subtle ways – these flower designs are from the ones on the cards, illustrating how using other colors or changing the number of stalks can alter the look of a quilled design.

Lavender

SUPPLIES

Base:

Dark brown wooden frame, 5" x 7"

Paper:

Quilling strips, ¼" – Purple/white variegated, purple, light purple

Quilling strips, ⅛" – Green

Dark green floral embossed paper, 5" x 7"

Cream card stock, 2½" x 3¾" and 2½" x ⅝"

Masking panel, 2¾" x 4" (Any card stock scrap will do.)

Tools & Other Supplies:

Basic supplies and tools for quilling

Brown marker

Inkpads – Gold, brown

Stencil brushes

Decorative label holder

Double-sided tape

INSTRUCTIONS

Make the Quilled Elements:

See the beginning of the book for detailed instructions.

1. Larger flower bud – (Make 16 in all.) Using ¼" purple/white variegated quilling strips, make bell shapes.

2. Smaller flower bud – (Make 10 in all.) Using ¼" light purple and purple quilling paper, make tight coils.
3. Green bud – (Make 6 in all.) Tear ⅛" green quilling strips into 3"

lengths. Make bell shapes.
4. Stem – (Make 2.) Cut a 4" length of ⅛" piece of quilling paper in half lengthwise.

Decorate & Assemble:

1. Color the edges of the cream card stock panels with brown ink.

2. Arrange the quilled elements, using the photo as a guide. Glue to the larger cream panel.

3. With a brown marker, write the botanical name of the plant (*Lavandula angustifolia*) on the smaller panel.

4. Use a small piece of double-sided tape, tape the masking panel on the green embossed paper panel. Using the stencil brush and gold ink, color along the edge of the masking panel, blending out towards the edge of the green paper, to create a frame for the panel with the quilled elements. See "Coloring Paper." Remove the masking panel.

5. Remove the glass and backing from the frame. Place the green panel in the frame. Replace the backing.

6. Glue the panel with the quilled elements in the middle of the rectangle created by the gold coloring.

7. Glue the smaller panel in the decorative label holder. Glue the label holder on the green paper, using the photo as a guide for placement. ❑

Framed Botanicals, continued from page 98

Foxglove

SUPPLIES

Base:

Dark brown wooden frame, 5" x 7"

Paper:

Quilling strips, ¼" – Blue/white variegated, purple/white variegated

Quilling strips, ⅛" – Green

Dark green floral embossed paper, 5" x 7"

Cream card stock, 2½" x 3¾" and 2½" x ⅝"

Masking panel, 2¾" x 4" (Any card stock scrap will do.)

Tools & Other Supplies:

Basic supplies and tools for quilling

Brown marker

Inkpads – Gold, brown

Stencil brushes

Decorative label holder

Double-sided tape

INSTRUCTIONS

Make the Quilled Elements:

See the beginning of the book for detailed instructions.

1. Blue flower – (Make 8.) Tear 12" of ¼" blue/white variegated quilling strips into 3", 3½" and 5½" lengths. Start quilling from the dark end and make bell shapes.

2. Purple flower – (Make 6.) Tear 12" of ¼" purple/white variegated quilling strips into 3", 3½" and 5½" lengths. Start quilling from the dark end and make bell shapes.

3. Bud – (Make 9 in all.) Tear ⅛" green quilling strips into 3" lengths. Make three bell shapes for the blue stem and six for the purple stem.

4. Leaf – (Make 11.) Cut ⅛" green quilling strips into 3" and 4" lengths. Make leaf shapes.

5. Stem – (Make 2.) Cut a 3" length of ⅛" green quilling paper in half lengthwise.

Decorate & Assemble:

1. Color the edges of the cream card stock panels with brown ink.

2. Arrange the quilled elements, using the photo as a guide. Place the smaller, darker blossoms at the top of the stem with the lighter and larger blossoms at the bottom. Glue to the larger cream panel.

3. With a brown marker, write the botanical name of the plant (*Digitalis purpurea*) on the smaller panel.

4. Use a small piece of double-sided tape, tape the masking panel on the green embossed paper panel. Using the stencil brush and gold ink, color along the edge of the masking panel, blending out towards the edge of the green paper, to create a frame for the panel with the quilled elements. See "Coloring Paper." Remove the masking panel.

5. Remove the glass and backing from the frame. Place the green panel in the frame. Replace the backing.

6. Glue the panel with the quilled elements in the middle of the rectangle created by the gold coloring.

7. Glue the smaller panel into the decorative label holder. Glue the label holder on the green paper, using the photo as a guide for placement. ❑

100

Hydrangea

SUPPLIES

Base:

Dark brown wooden frame, 5" x 7"

Paper:

Quilling strips, ⅛" – Green

Dark green floral embossed paper, 5" x 7"

Cream card stock

Green card stock

Masking panel, 2¾" x 4" (Any card stock scrap will do.)

Tools & Other Supplies:

Decorative punches – Blossom, 1" diameter; leaf, ¾" x ½"

Embossing pad

Embossing tool

Brown marker

Inkpads – Green, purple, gold, brown

Stencil brushes

Decorative label holder

Double-sided tape

Seed beads

White glue

Tweezers

INSTRUCTIONS

Make the Paper Flowers:

See the "Making Shaped Paper."

1. From the cream card stock, cut two panels, one 2½" x 3¾" and one 2½" x ⅝".
2. Using stencil brushes, color part of the remaining cream card stock with the inks, blending the green into the purple. See "Coloring Paper."
3. Punch 12 small blossoms from the ink-colored paper.
4. Shape the blossoms on the embossing pad.
5. Using white glue, adhere a seed bead in the center of each blossom.
6. Color the green card stock with purple ink, using a stencil brush.

7. Punch five leaves from the inked green card stock.
8. Shape the leaves on the embossing pad.

Decorate & Assemble:

1. Color the edges of the cream card stock panels with brown ink.
2. Arrange the blossoms in a dome shape towards the top of the larger cream panel, placing the flowers so the colors blend one into the other.
3. Cut four stems, each 3" long, from ⅛" green quilling paper.
4. Working one strip at a time, dip the one end of the strip in white glue and position in the blossoms. Let dry completely.
5. Glue the stems together and glue in place on the card. Trim the ends even with the bottom of the card.
6. With a brown marker, write the botanical name of the plant (*Hydrangea macrophylla*) on the smaller panel.
7. Use a small piece of double-sided tape, tape the masking panel on the green embossed paper panel. Using the stencil brush and gold ink, color along the edge of the masking panel, blending out towards the edge of the green paper, to create a frame for the panel with the quilled elements. See "Coloring Paper." Remove the masking panel.
8. Remove the glass and backing from the frame. Place the green panel in the frame. Replace the backing.
9. Glue the panel with the flowers in the middle of the rectangle created by the gold coloring.
10. Glue the shaped leaves in place, using the photo as a guide for placement and allowing them to hang over the edge of the panel.
11. Glue the smaller panel into the decorative label holder. Glue the label holder on the green paper, using the photo as a guide for placement. ❏

Framed Critters

Brightly colored critters, mounted in a four-window frame, make a cheerful decoration for a child's room. The husked shapes have leafy backgrounds made from colored card stock trimmed with pinking scissors. See pages 108 and 109 for patterns for leaves and grasses and the beginning of the book for detailed instructions on husking and quilling. Individual instructions for each critter follow these General Instructions.

General Supplies

Base:

Wooden window frame, 14" square with four 5¼" square windows

Acrylic paint – Medium blue

Acrylic varnish, satin finish

Backing board, 12" square (I used a canvas board; you could cut a piece of mat board instead.)

Papers:

Bright blue paper, four 5½" squares

Bright green card stock

Green card stock

Tools & Other Supplies:

Patterns for leaves and grass

Decorative edge scissors – Pinking

Iridescent watercolors and applicator

Glue stick

Double-sided tape

General Instructions

1. Paint the frame with medium blue paint. Let dry.
2. Apply varnish. Let dry.
3. Using the leaf and grass patterns provided, cut out the leaf and grass shapes from bright green card stock.
4. Using a glue stick, glue the shapes on green card stock. Cut around the shapes with pinking scissors, leaving a narrow border.
5. Glue the leaf and grass shapes on the bright blue paper panels, using

the photo as a guide for placement.

6. With double-sided tape, secure the blue panels in the window frame.
7. Attach the backboard to the frame with white glue.
8. Make the husked critters (individual instructions for each critter follow) and glue each to the appropriate background in the frame, using the photo as a guide for placement.
9. Using the iridescent watercolors and applicator, color each top edge of the critters' wings and inner body pieces. ❏

Ladybug

SUPPLIES

Papers:

Quilling strips, ¼" – Green, red, black

Red card stock

Tools & Other Supplies:

Basic supplies and tools for quilling

Basic supplies and tools for husking (See "Husking.")

Decorative edge scissors – Pinking

PATTERN

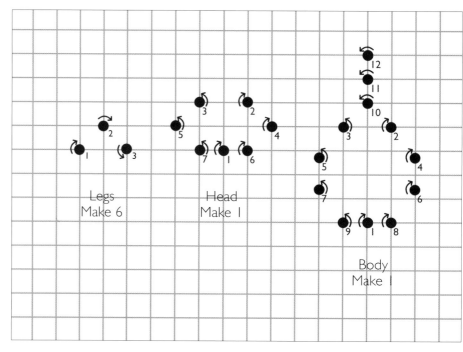

Legs
Make 6

Head
Make 1

Body
Make 1

Ladybug, continued

INSTRUCTIONS

1. Main body piece – (Make 1.) Glue the ends of a ¼" green quilling strip and a ¼" red quilling strip together. Follow the husking pattern using the two strips. Using ¼" red quilling strips, make the three extra collars on the body piece.

2. After forming the body piece, glue it on red card stock. Cut around the shape with pinking scissors.

3. Foot – (Make 6.) Use ¼" black quilling strips and follow the husking pattern.

4. Black dot – (Make 6.) Tear ¼" black quilling strips into 3" lengths. Make tight coils.

5. Head – (Make 1.) Use ¼" black quilling strips and follow the husking pattern.

6. Feelers – (Make 1.) Cut a 6" length of ¼" black quilling paper. Make a T-scroll.

7. Glue the ladybug to the pointed leaf panel at lower right part of the frame. ❏

Continued on page 104.

Frog

SUPPLIES

Papers:

Quilling strips, ¼" – Dark green, green, red, white, black

Green card stock

Tools & Other Supplies:

Basic supplies and tools for quilling

Basic supplies and tools for husking (See "Husking.")

Decorative edge scissors – Pinking

2 googly eyes

INSTRUCTIONS

1. Body – (Make 1.) Glue the ends of a ¼" green quilling strip and a ¼" dark green quilling strip together. Follow the husking pattern, using the two strips for the main body piece. Use ¼" green quilling strips for the three extra collars on the body piece.

2. After forming the body piece, glue it on green card stock. Cut around the shape with pinking scissors.

3. Frog leg and foot – (Make 4 of each.) Use ¼" green quilling strips and follow the husking patterns.

4. Eyes – (Make 2.) Tear ¼" green quilling strips into 3" lengths. Make loose coils. Glue a googly eye on top of each coil.

5. Tongue – (Make 1.) Cut a 3" of ¼" red quilling paper. Make a single scroll.

6. Fly – (Make 1 or more.) Tear a 6" piece of black quilling paper and make a tight coil. Tear 3" lengths of white quilling strips and make two teardrop shapes.

7. Arrange the husked frog pieces as shown in the project photo or try one of the options, *pictured opposite.*

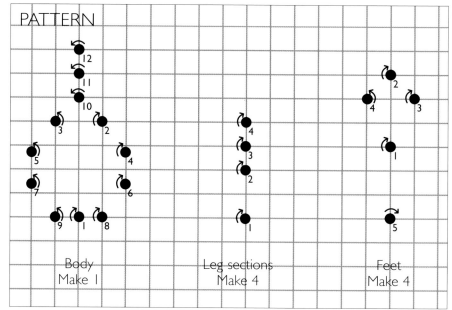

PATTERN

Body
Make 1

Leg sections
Make 4

Feet
Make 4

Use all four leg sections for the back legs. Cut additional pieces of quilling strips for the front legs.

8. Glue the frog and fly on the panel with the lily pad shaped leaf on the lower left window of the frame. ❑

Other Frog Arrangements

After you've made the quilled or husked elements for a project, you can experiment with arranging the elements and how you glue them together. For example, husked frog elements can be arranged and glued together so the frog is sitting or jumping and swimming. The feet of the middle frog were wrapped with a finishing hoop to create a variation. You can also change the look of the tongue (or have no tongue), add more flies, or substitute another bug.

Framed Critters, Continued from page 104

Bee

SUPPLIES

Papers:

Quilling strips, ¼" – Black, cream, yellow

Yellow card stock

Tools & Other Supplies:

Basic supplies and tools for quilling

Basic supplies and tools for husking (See "Husking.")

Decorative edge scissors – Pinking

INSTRUCTIONS

1. Larger body segment – (Make 1.) Glue together the ends of a ¼" black quilling strip and a ¼" yellow quilling strip. Follow the husking pattern, using the two strips.

2. After forming the larger body segment, glue it to yellow card stock. Cut around the shape with pinking scissors.

3. Smaller body segment – (Make 1.) Tear an 8" length of black quilling paper. Make one loose coil.

4. Wing – (Make 2.) Use ¼" cream quilling strips and follow the husking pattern.

5. Head – (Make 1.) Use ¼" black quilling paper and follow the husking pattern. When finished, pinch the head piece to form a point on the outside collar.

6. Feelers – (Make 1.) Cut a 4" piece of ¼" black quilling paper. Make a feeler scroll.

7. Arrange the elements, using the photo as a guide, and glue in the upper right window of the frame over the multiple blades of grass. ❏

PATTERN

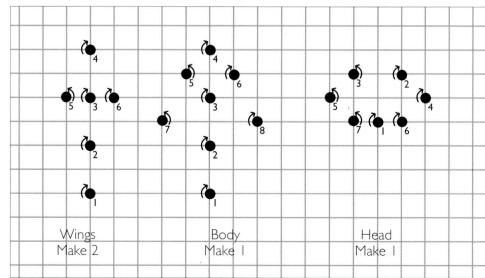

Wings
Make 2

Body
Make 1

Head
Make 1

Dragonfly

SUPPLIES

Papers:

Quilling strips, ¼" – Pink, bright green

Bright pink card stock

Tools & Other Supplies:

Basic supplies and tools for quilling

Basic supplies and tools for husking (See "Husking.")

Decorative edge scissors – Pinking

2 small circular iridescent sequin stickers

INSTRUCTIONS

1. Body – Following the husking pattern, make four loops with a green quilling strip and the remaining loops with a pink quilling strip.
2. Wings – (Make 2 of each type.) Glue together the ends of a ¼" green quilling strip and a ¼" pink quilling strip. Follow the husking pattern, using the two strips. Make 2 large wings and 2 small wings.
3. After forming and gluing the two pairs of wings together, glue each pair on pink paper. Cut around each shape with pinking scissors.
4. Eyes and accent – (Make 3 in all.) Tear ¼" green quilling strips into 6" lengths. Make tight coils. Add an iridescent sequin sticker to two of the coils. (These will be the eyes.)
5. Feelers – (Make 1.) Cut a 3" piece of green quilling paper. Make a feeler scroll
6. Using the photo as a guide, arrange the pieces and glue to the upper right panel – the one with the single blade of grass. ❑

HUSKING PATTERNS

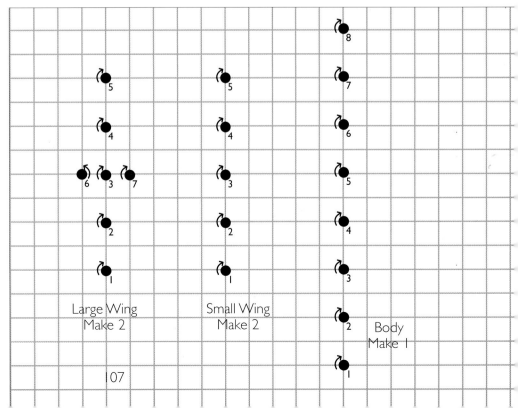

Large Wing
Make 2

Small Wing
Make 2

Body
Make 1

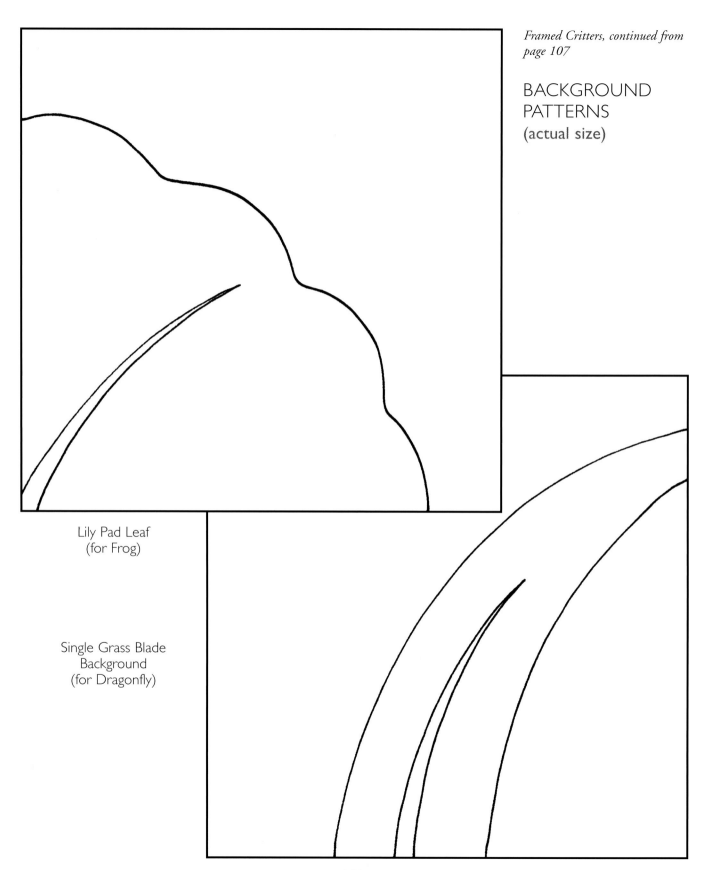

Framed Critters, continued from page 107

BACKGROUND PATTERNS
(actual size)

Lily Pad Leaf
(for Frog)

Single Grass Blade
Background
(for Dragonfly)

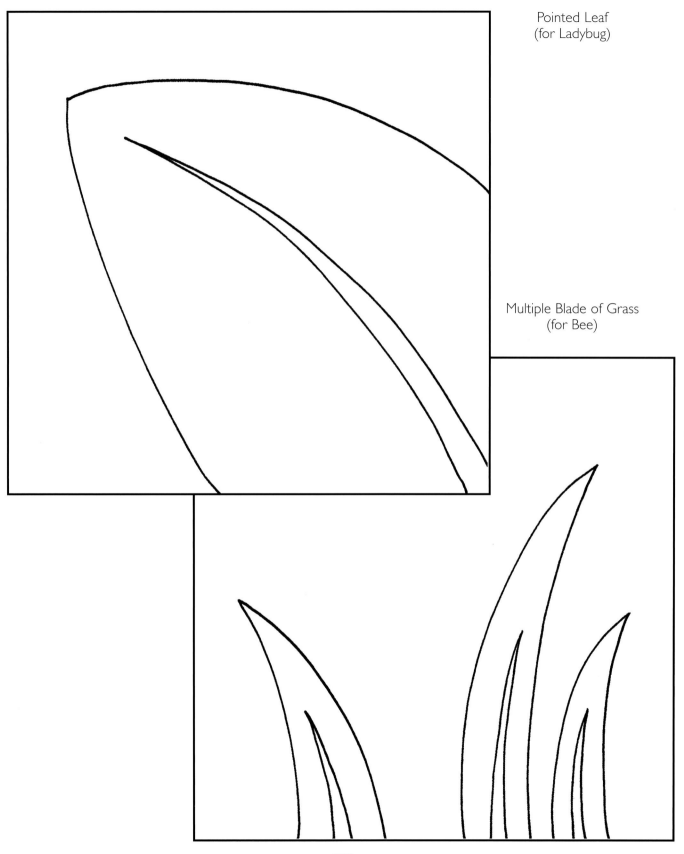

Pointed Leaf
(for Ladybug)

Multiple Blade of Grass
(for Bee)

Blue Butterfly

This husked butterfly has an open filigree appearance that's easy and fast to make.
A rub-on saying was applied to the background paper before the butterfly was glued in place.

SUPPLIES

Base:

White shadow box frame, 6" square,
1¾" deep

Papers:

Quilling strips, ¼" – Two-toned
(blue and white)

Quilling strips, ⅛" – Blue

White card stock, 5½" square

Tools & Other Supplies:

Basic supplies and tools for quilling

Basic supplies and tools for husking
(See "Husking.")

Blue inkpad

Stencil brush

Rub-on saying

PATTERN

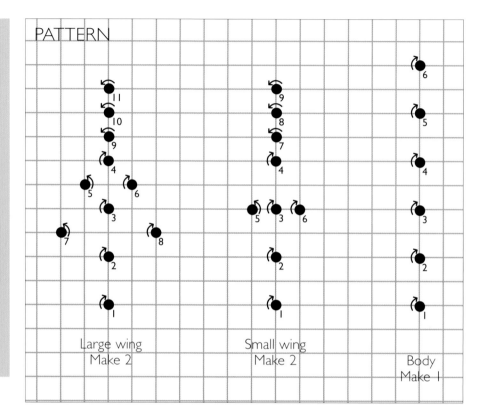

Large wing
Make 2

Small wing
Make 2

Body
Make 1

INSTRUCTIONS

Make the Husked Butterfly:

See "Husking" for detailed instructions.

1. Body – (Make 1.) Use ¼" two-toned quilling strips and follow the husking pattern. Start with the blue side of the quilling strip on the outside of the loops. When finished, gently pinch and curve the bottom of the body.

2. Large wings – (Make 2.) Use ¼" two-toned quilling strips and follow the husking pattern. Start with the blue side of the quilling strip on the outside of the loops. Follow the pattern and loop and collar the shape after the #8 pin. Trim off any excess paper. Crimp the quilling strips

before you make the #9, #10, and #11 collar pieces. Pinch the top of the #11 collar to form the wing.

3. Small wings – (Make 2.) Use ¼" two-toned quilling strips and follow the husking pattern. When husking, start with the blue side of the quilling strip on the outside of the loops. Follow the pattern and loop and collar the shape after the #6 pin. Trim off the excess paper. Crimp the quilling strips for the #7, #8, and #9 collar pieces.

4. Glue the large wings to the small wings.

Make the Quilled Shapes:

See the beginning of the book for detailed instructions.

Feelers – (Make 1.) Cut a 6" piece of ⅛" blue quilling paper. Make a feeler scroll.

Decorate & Assemble:

1. Color the edges of the white card panel with blue ink, using a stencil brush.

2. Add the rub-on saying to the bottom of the panel.

3. Glue the husked butterfly on the colored blue panel. Glue the wings at an angle, to create dimension.

4. Glue the butterfly feelers in place.

5. Insert the panel in the frame. ❏

Go confidently in the direction of your dreams. Live the life you have imagined.

Monarch Butterfly with Purple Flower

This monarch butterfly, which hovers over a quilled petaled flower, shows how husked shapes can be further accented and enhanced by filling in the open spaces with quilled pieces. Because it's shown in a side view, the butterfly has only one set of wings.

SUPPLIES

Base:

White shadow box frame, 6" square, 1¾" deep

Papers:

Quilling strips, ¼" – Black, orange, yellow, purple, green

Quilling strips, ⅛" – Black

White card stock panel, 5½" square

Tools & Other Supplies:

Basic supplies and tools for quilling

Basic supplies and tools for husking

Blue inkpad

Stencil brush

INSTRUCTIONS

Make the Husked Butterfly:

See "Husking" for detailed instructions.

1. Body – (Make 1.) Use ¼" black quilling strips and follow the husking pattern. When finished, gently pinch and curve the bottom of the body.
2. Large wing – (Make 1.) Use ¼" black and orange quilling strips and follow the husking pattern. Loop and collar the shape after the #8 pin. Trim off any excess paper. Crimp the orange quilling strip for the #9 collar. Trim off the excess paper. Crimp the black quilling strips for the #10 and #11 collar pieces. Pinch the top of the #11 collar to form the wing.
3. Small wing – (Make 1.) Use ¼"

black and orange quilling strips. Follow the husking pattern and loop and collar the shape after the #6 pin. Trim off any excess paper. Crimp the orange quilling strip for the extra #7 collar. Trim off excess paper. Crimp the black quilling strips for the #8 and #9 collar pieces.
4. Glue the large wing to the small wing.

Make the Quilled Shapes for the Butterfly:

See the beginning of the book for detailed instructions.

1. Feelers – (Make 1.) Cut a 6" length of ⅛" black quilling paper. Make a feeler scroll.
2. With black ¼" quilling strips, make:

   3 loose coils with 2" lengths

   2 teardrops with 4" lengths

   4 teardrops with 3" lengths

   5 teardrops with 2" lengths
3. With orange ¼" quilling strips, make:

   3 loose coils with 3" lengths

   4 teardrops with 4" lengths

   2 teardrops with 2" lengths
4. With yellow ¼" quilling strips, make:

   2 loose coils with 3" lengths

   2 teardrops with 3" lengths

   1 teardrop with a 2" length

Make the Purple Flower:

See the beginning of the book for detailed instructions.

1. Center – (Make 1.) Tear a 12" length of ¼" yellow quilling paper. Make a half moon shape.
2. Petal – (Make 7 in all.) Use ¼" purple quilling strips and husk 7 wheatears – one with six loops, four with five loops, one with four loops, and one with three loops. See "Husking."
3. Leaf – (Make 1.) Use ¼" green quilling strips and follow the husking pattern for the bee's wing. Pinch the top loop into a point to make the leaf shape.
4. Stem – Glue two ¼" green quilling strips together. Cut one 3" piece and one 2" piece.

Decorate & Assemble:

1. Color the edges of the white card panel with blue ink, using a stencil brush.
2. Glue the quilled orange, black, and yellow shapes into the husked wings, using the photo of the project as a guide.
3. Arrange and glue the husked butterfly on the colored blue panel.
4. Glue the butterfly feelers in place.
5. Arrange the pieces of the purple flower, using the photo as a guide. Glue in place with the stems on edge and attached to the leaf and between the petals of the flower. Trim the ends of the stem so the panel fits in the frame.
6. Insert the panel in the frame. ❏

Flower Place Markers

The wider (⅜") quilling paper is especially nice to use if you have trouble seeing or manipulating the thinner-width papers, and it's excellent for creating larger shapes.

These fresh spring flowers can be used as table decorations and, by writing a person's name on the stem, as place markers. They do not take long to make but will make a lasting impression at your next celebration. They'd also make a nice hostess gift, presented in a shallow, flat box.

SUPPLIES

Papers:

Quilling strips, ⅜" – Green, purple, red, blue

Tools & Other Supplies:

Basic supplies and tools for quilling

Basic supplies and tools for husking

Scissors

Black fine-tip marker

INSTRUCTIONS

Make the Quilled & Husked Elements:

See the beginning of the book for detailed instructions.

Iris

1. Central petals – Use purple ⅜" quilling paper, full length. Make a husking wheatear with seven loops spaced ⅜" apart.
2. Side petals – Cut a 6" length of ⅜" purple quilling paper. Quill into V-scroll.
3. Calyx – Cut a 6" length of ⅜" green quilling paper. Quill into an oval shape.
4. Stem – Cut two 6" lengths of ⅜" green quilling paper. Quill into single scrolls.

Rosebud

1. Bud – Use ⅜" red quilling paper, full length. Make an eccentric coil and pinch into a teardrop shape.
2. Side petals – Cut a 6" length of ⅜" red quilling paper. Quill into a V-scroll.
3. Calyx – Cut a 6" length of ⅜" green quilling paper. Quill into a loose coil.
4. Stem – Cut two 6" lengths of ⅜" green quilling paper. Quill into single scrolls.

Bluebell

1. Flower – Use ⅜" blue quilling paper, full length. Make an eccentric coil and pinch into a heart shape but without the bottom pinch so the shape resembles a tulip.
2. Side petals – Cut a 6" length of ⅜" blue quilling paper. Quill into V-scroll.
3. Calyx – Cut a 6" length of ⅜" green quilling paper. Quill into a half moon shape.
4. Stem – Cut two 6" lengths of ⅜" green quilling paper. Quill into single scrolls.

Continued on page 116

Flower Place Markers, continued from page 114

Assemble:

After the elements are made, the construction is the same for each.

1. Glue the side petals to the flower. Use the photo as a guide for placement – the spacing on each flower is slightly different.
2. Attach the calyx to the base of the flower.
3. Glue the single scrolls to the base along the sides of the flower and calyx. Leave the bottom piece straight for the stem, and quill the top piece into a single scroll to resemble a leaf.
4. Finish by writing the name of the guest on the stem with a fine-tip marker. ❏

Quilled Fridge Magnets

A little fine glitter is added to the epoxy casting resin before pouring it over
the quilled pieces, adding sparkle to these bright and cheerful magnets.
The resin makes them sturdy and imparts a transparent effect to
the paper. Make as many at a time as your mold will hold.

SUPPLIES

Papers:

Quilling strips, ⅜" – Variegated, in various colors

Quilling strips, ⅛" – Matching colors

Scraps of card stock – Matching colors (for punched flowers)

Dark green card stock

Tools & Other Supplies:

Basic supplies and tools for quilling

Scissors *or* fringing tool

Decorative punches – Daisy, 1" diameter; leaf, ½"

Two-part epoxy casting resin

Resin mold with 1¼" circular cavities

Clear iridescent fine glitter

Magnetic sheet

INSTRUCTIONS

Make the Fringed Flower:

See "Making Fringed Flowers" for detailed instructions.

Fringed flower – (Make 1 per magnet.) Cut a 6" length of ⅜" variegated quilling paper. Glue a 3" strip of ⅛" quilling paper to the end to create the center. Form the flower.

Punch the Leaves & Background Blossom:

1. Leaves – (Make 2 for each magnet.) Punch two leaves from green card stock. Shape the leaves on an embossing pad.
2. Background blossom – (Make 1 per magnet.) Using the daisy punch, punch one blossom from matching card stock.

Assemble:

1. Using white glue, glue two leaves to the fringed flower.
2. Glue the fringed flower to the punched daisy. Let the glue dry completely before proceeding.
3. Following the package instructions, mix two ounces casting resin. Add a small amount of glitter to the mixed resin and mix well.
4. Pour a few drops of resin in the mold cavity. Place the flower in the cavity. Pour the resin over the paper sculpture to a depth of ¼" in each cavity.
5. Let the resin cure completely. Remove from the mold.
6. Cut one 1" diameter circle from the magnet sheet for each piece. Use white glue to attach the magnet to the bottom of the cast piece. ❏

Quilled Jewelry Projects

Quilled pieces make wonderful paper jewelry. The pieces are colorful, lightweight, and inexpensive, and you can combine different paper colors to coordinate with your clothes for a custom look.

A concern, however, is protecting the pieces from moisture and wear. The projects in this section show various ways to protect paper jewelry pieces: embedding them in a two-part epoxy casting resin, spraying with clear varnish, or applying a clear dimensional varnish coating.

Fringed Flower Pendant

A small tag base and matte spray sealer are used to make quilled shapes into a wearable piece of art. Rolling different colors and widths of quilling strips around a wooden toothpick makes the beads. (Using a toothpick creates a larger hole so the beads are easier to work with.)

SUPPLIES

Papers:

Quilling strips, ⅜" – Blue/white variegated

Quilling strips, ⅛" – Blue/white variegated, green/white variegated,

Quilling strips, ¼" – Blue, green

Lime green with white polka dots card stock

Jewelry Supplies & Findings:

1 large clear rhinestone

3 tiny silver eyelets

2 silver head pins, 2" long

Clear seed beads

1 silver tag charm

3 silver jump rings

1⅓ yds. silver cord

Jewelry clasp

Tools & Other Supplies:

Basic supplies and tools for quilling

Round wooden toothpicks

Scissors *or* fringing tool

Clear matte spray

Piece of plastic foam

Roundnose pliers

Hole punch *or* awl

INSTRUCTIONS

Make the Quilled Elements:

See the beginning of the book for detailed instructions.

1. Fringed flower – (Make 1.) Cut a 6" length of ⅜" blue/white quilling paper. Glue a 6" length of ⅛" blue quilling paper on the end for the center. See "Making Fringed Flowers."

2. Large paisley – (Make 1.) Cut a 10" length of ⅛" white/green quilling paper. Make an eccentric coil. Pinch the glued end to make a petal shape.

3. Small paisley – (Make 3.) Cut 3" lengths of ⅛" of blue/white quilling paper. Make petal shapes. Use tweezers to curl the end of each one to make the paisley shape.

4. Scroll – (Make 1.) Cut a 2" length of ⅛" white/green quilling paper. Make a single scroll.

5. Beads – (Make 4 in all.) On a round wooden toothpick, roll and glue the various quilling strips to form bead shapes of different sizes. Use the photo as a guide.

Assemble:

1. Cut the lime green card stock to make a tag 2" x 1⅛".

2. Glue the quilled paisley elements and the fringed flower on the tag, using the photo as a guide.

3. Cut a 2" length of ¼" green quilling paper and form a tight coil on a wooden toothpick. Glue at the top of the tag behind the fringed flower. (The silver cord will be threaded through this piece.)

4. Place the quilled beads on toothpicks and push into a piece of plastic foam.

5. Spray the tag with the flower and paisleys and the beads with several coats of the clear varnish. Protect your work surface and work in a well-ventilated area. Let dry between coats.

6. Thread a seed bead on each head pin. Then thread the quilled beads and more seed beads on the head pins, finishing with seed beads. Using round nose pliers, form the top of each pin into a loop.

7. Make three small holes along the bottom of the tag. Install the eyelets.

8. Using jump rings, attach the silver tag charm and beaded head pins to the tag.

9. Thread the silver cord through the top of the tag and add the clasp to the ends to the cord.

10. Glue the rhinestone in the center of the fringed flower. ❏

Flower Power
Pendant & Earrings

Lightly spraying clear matte varnish on both sides of these quilled pieces make them sturdy and wearable. The necklace is a five-petal flower; the earrings have three petals and are suspended on lengths of fine silver chain.

SUPPLIES

Papers:

Quilling strips, ⅛" – Light blue, brown

Scrap of dark brown card stock

Jewelry Supplies & Findings:

5 brown rhinestones

⅔ yd. brown and blue narrow ribbon

Silver clasp

8" fine silver chain

Two silver earring posts

Tools & Other Supplies:

Basic supplies and tools for quilling

Decorative punch – Flower, 1" diameter

Clear matte sealer spray

Wire cutters

INSTRUCTIONS

Make the Flowers:

1. Pendant petals – (Make 10 in all.) Tear 8" lengths of blue quilling strips. Make five eccentric teardrop shapes. Cut 10" lengths of brown quilling strips. Make five eccentric teardrop shapes.
2. Earring petals – (Make 6.) Tear 6" lengths of blue quilling strips. Make eccentric teardrop shapes.
3. Earring tops – (Make 2.) Tear 4" lengths of brown quilling strips. Make half moon shapes.

Assemble:

1. Punch a flower from brown card stock. (It will be the base for the pendant petals.)
2. Glue the quilled elements together to form the flower pendant and earrings. For the pendant, glue the blue petals together to make a flower. Then glue the brown petals together to make a second flower. Glue the brown quilled flower on the brown punched flower. Glue the blue quilled flower on top.
3. Tear three 2" lengths of ⅛" brown quilling strips. Form three tight coils on a wooden toothpick.
4. Glue one tight coil at the top of the pendant and one to the top of each earring. (The chains and jump ring will be threaded through these pieces.)
5. Working in a well-ventilated area, spray the pendant and the earring pieces with several coats of clear sealer. Let dry.
6. Attach a jump ring to the coil on the flower pendant and thread the ribbon through the jump ring. Attach the clasp pieces to the ends of the ribbon.
7. Cut the chain into two 4" pieces. Thread a length of chain through each earring. Attach the ends of one chain to a jump ring, then to an earring post. Repeat to make the other earring.
8. Glue a rhinestone at the center of the flower pendant. Glue a rhinestone on each side of both earrings for sparkle. ❏

Pink & Yellow Flower Pendants

This colorful quilled flower is encased in a clear epoxy casting resin to make a fun, durable pendant. This is a terrific way to use quilled elements left over from card making. You can make several at a time – as many as your mold has cavities. Scratches can be buffed away with car wax and a soft cloth.

Pink Flower Pendant

SUPPLIES

Papers:

Quilling strips, ⅛" – Light green, yellow, pink

Jewelry Supplies & Findings:

Large silver pinch bail

Silver chain

Tools & Other Supplies:

Basic supplies and tools for quilling

Needlenose pliers

Two-part epoxy casting resin

Resin mold with 1" x 1½" rectangular cavities

Drill with ¹⁄₁₆" bit

INSTRUCTIONS

Make the Quilled Flower:

See the beginning of the book for detailed instructions.

1. Flower petal – (Make 5.) Tear 4" lengths of pink quilling strips. Make teardrop shapes.
2. Center – (Make 1.) Tear a 3" length of yellow quilling paper. Make a tight coil shape.
3. Leaf – (Make 2.) Tear 4" lengths of light green quilling strips. Make leaf shapes.
4. Scroll – (Make 2.) Cut 2" lengths of light green quilling strips. Make single scrolls.

Assemble:

1. Glue the quilled elements together to form the flower. Let the glue dry completely before proceeding.
2. Place the quilled pieces in a mold cavity.
3. Following the package instructions, mix two ounces of casting resin.
4. Pour the resin over the paper sculpture, filling the cavity with the resin.
5. Let the resin cure completely. Remove from the mold.
6. Drill a small hole in the top of the pendant. Attach the bail and string on a chain. ❏

Yellow Flower Pendant

SUPPLIES

Papers:

Quilling strips, ⅛" – Bright green, dark green, yellow, red

Jewelry Supplies & Findings:

Large silver pinch bail

Silver chain

Tools & Other Supplies:

Basic supplies and tools for quilling

Needlenose cutters

Two-part epoxy casting resin

Resin mold with 1" x 1½" rectangular cavities

Drill with ¹⁄₁₆" bit

INSTRUCTIONS

Make the Quilled Elements:

See the beginning of the book for detailed instructions.

1. Flower petal – (Make 7.) Tear 4" lengths of yellow quilling strips. Make teardrop shapes.
2. Center – (Make 1.) Tear a 3" piece of red quilling paper. Make a tight coil.
3. Leaf – (Make 2.) Tear 4" lengths of bright green quilling strips. Make leaf shapes.
4. Scroll – (Make 2.) Cut 2" lengths of dark green quilling strips. Make single scrolls.

Assemble:

1. Glue the quilled elements together to form the flower. Let the glue dry completely before proceeding.
2. Place the quilled pieces in a mold cavity.
3. Following the package instructions, mix two ounces of casting resin.
4. Pour the resin over the paper sculpture, filling the cavity with the resin.
5. Let the resin cure completely. Remove from the mold.
6. Drill a small hole in the top of the pendant. Attach the bail and string on a chain. ❏

Heart Pendant

Another way to protect a quilled piece is with dimensional clear varnish. Make sure the paper pieces are securely glued down before coating with the varnish or they will warp. This very simple, fun piece of jewelry could be made to match a summer outfit.

SUPPLIES

Papers:
Quilling strips, ⅛" – Bright pink

Jewelry Supplies & Findings:
1 silver pendant with recessed area
1 silver jump ring
⅔ yd. thin green and pink ribbon
Silver clasp

Tools & Other Supplies:
Basic supplies and tools for quilling
Light blue acrylic paint
Clear dimensional varnish

INSTRUCTIONS

Make the Quilled Elements:
See the beginning of the book for detailed instructions.
Heart – Tear two 6" lengths of ⅛" pink quilling paper. Make 2 petal shapes.

Assemble:
1. Paint the recessed area of the pendant with the light blue paint. Let dry completely.
2. Coat the painted area with clear dimensional varnish. Let dry.
3. Glue the petals shapes together to form the heart. Glue them on the pendant. Let dry completely.
4. Coat the top of the heart with two coats of clear dimensional varnish. Let the first coat dry completely before adding the second coat.
5. Attach the ribbon to the pendant, using a jump ring.
6. Attach the clasp pieces to the ends of the ribbon. ❑

Metric Conversion Chart

Inches to Millimeters and Centimeters

Inches	MM	CM	Inches	MM	CM
1/8	3	.3	2	51	5.1
1/4	6	.6	3	76	7.6
3/8	10	1.0	4	102	10.2
1/2	13	1.3	5	127	12.7
5/8	16	1.6	6	152	15.2
3/4	19	1.9	7	178	17.8
7/8	22	2.2	8	203	20.3
1	25	2.5	9	229	22.9
1-1/4	32	3.2	10	254	25.4
1-1/2	38	3.8	11	279	27.9
1-3/4	44	4.4	12	305	30.5

Yards to Meters

Yards	Meters	Yards	Meters
1/8	.11	3	2.74
1/4	.23	4	3.66
3/8	.34	5	4.57
1/2	.46	6	5.49
5/8	.57	7	6.40
3/4	.69	8	7.32
7/8	.80	9	8.23
1	.91	10	9.14
2	1.83		

Index

Continued on next page